With Only the Beat
of My Heart

To my comrade

J. David Hoge

With Only the Beat of My Heart

An Immigrant's Journey to and through America

I. DAVID HONG MD,
US NAVY CAPTAIN, RETIRED

Copyright © 2008 by I. David Hong MD, US Navy Captain, Retired.

Library of Congress Control Number: 2008902597
ISBN: Hardcover 978-1-4363-3054-1
Softcover 978-1-4363-3053-4

All rights reserved. No part of this book may be reproduced or transmitted in any form or by any means, electronic or mechanical, including photocopying, recording, or by any information storage and retrieval system, without permission in writing from the copyright owner.

This book was printed in the United States of America.

To order additional copies of this book, contact:
Xlibris Corporation
1-888-795-4274
www.Xlibris.com
Orders@Xlibris.com

Contents

	Introduction	vii
1.	Old World Roots	1
2.	Motherless Years	6
3.	The Civil War: Chaos and Blood on the Streets	9
4.	Survival is Victory	13
5.	The Search for Corned Beef and the Return of Peace	19
6.	My Mother Returns after Seven Years	25
7.	Rites of Passage	28
8.	Transpacific Passage	30
9.	Escape!	33
10.	A New Life at the Spanish American Institute, and Orphanage	39
11.	The Smell of Hard-earned Money	43
12.	Devastating Disappointment	46
13.	The Doors Begin to Open	49
14.	College Days	53
15.	My first Job in Science	56
16.	Among the Migrant Ministry	58
17.	Out to Find America	62
18.	My First Return to Korea: Rediscovering the Stories	69
19.	Vanderbilt Medical School	78
20.	Marriage	84
21.	Julie Gives Us a Scare	89
22.	Life on the Farm	93
23.	Trouble on the Farm and the "Man in Black"	96
24.	Kim Arrives: the Love of My Life	99
25.	Dangerous Duty in Korea	102
26.	I Am David	106
27.	Washington State and Another Tour of Duty	108
28.	A Bad Business Deal	111
29.	Mission in Guatemala	114
30.	Reflections of an "Elder"	117

Introduction

David Hong, a descendant of high officials of the ancient Korean Kingdom, dating possibly as far back as the invasion of Genghis Khan, tells of growing up with his father and sisters in Seoul before, during, and after the Korean War. Having suffered the abandonment of his mother, followed by the bombing and evacuation of Seoul in 1950, he and his father negotiate the streets and countryside of a brutal and desperate country, trying to survive. He recounts the terrors he witnessed during a relentless war, periods of near starvation, sometimes-hostile Communist soldiers, and the collapse of a nation. During this period, he forms a precious bond with his enigmatic father in whom they provide each other with protection as his father flees from mandatory military conscription and tries to barter goods to feed the family. Young Inpow Hong (his given name) develops an increased fascination with America during this time, as it is seen as the liberator of Seoul and the architect of industrial power; and before long, he finds himself an immigrant orphan in Southern California.

After a bitter divorce of his mother (who finally returns after seven years) and father, agree to send him to California at the age of 16 from the Pusan Harbor dock in Korea, along with his younger sister, to live with arranged adoptive parents near Los Angeles. He arrives with only the gift of two antique vases and a $100 bill carefully sewn by his father into the lining of his jacket in case of emergency. After sadly leaving his sister at a Los Angeles orphanage and trying to conform to the lifestyle of his new home, possessing very little English, Young Hong sees the inevitable limitations, abuse, and lifelessness that await him in his adoptive home and sends a red-ink SOS letter to his father in Korea asking him to understand why he must flee.

He then sneaks away on a bus and hits the streets of the Sunset Strip in Hollywood, taking his chances as a refugee with only a few dollars of saved milk money in his pocket. After a humiliating compulsory return to his adoptive parents, his wish is fulfilled to be sent to an orphanage where he continues his education and assimilation into American society, quickly distinguishing himself from the majority of the other boys and young men at the Spanish American Institute orphanage near Los Angeles.

What stands out as we witness his amazing adaptability is Hong's unusual capacity to foresee the future and maintain a sense of personal destiny while in a position of extreme vulnerability in a strange country. We are reminded of the importance of first-born sons in Korea; and Young Inpow retains this sense of importance, even as an orphan in the United States with virtually no one to guide him, though allies (often unseen) continually and auspiciously appear as he persists in pursuing his dream of becoming a doctor.

His relentless ambition, willingness to learn, assimilate and advance in the new world eventually brings him to medical school, prestigious positions, and accomplishments as a respected psychiatrist, an officer in the US Navy and Army, then retiring as a Colonel. This Horatio Alger-like story is a classic document of hope outlasting despair and misfortune as the hero, a self-made man possessing an indomitable constitution, born into and dispossessed from one of the most prestigious families in Korea overcomes a variety of disappointments and obstacles, always landing on his feet. David Hong thereby succeeds in finding the true American dream, demonstrating that hard work, faith, and determination can deliver a disadvantaged immigrant to a world of opportunity and, eventually, after two failed marriages, a happy home.

In Hong's memoir, we find many paradoxes at the heart of his peculiar immigrant experience. A boy from one of the wealthiest families in Korea becomes completely dispossessed, impoverished, and anonymous. We see him officially naturalize as a citizen of the US, as a conscientious objector, having witnessed one of the bloodiest wars of the modern era, eventually to become a distinguished officer in the US Army and Navy, as a physician in his native Korea—including dangerous duty in the volatile DMZ. We see a boy and a young man who loves his native land unable to find a place in it, returning years later as an American, having found the country he loved even more, and upon returning to Seoul, a true companion in a traditional Korean woman. He also takes us along the highways and often-unseen communities and subcultures of America, where as a young immigrant missionary, he takes vivid interest in every person he meets, displaying uncommon sympathy for all walks of life, and a voracious appetite for intellectual discourse. Yet, all the while, he feels the absence of his Korean father, to whom he remains deeply bound, even amid the great distance between them. Though family conflicts follow him, they are always resolved in his deep love of country and his identity as an American.

As we witness this journey, we feel an isolation and longing accompanied by a string of worldly accomplishments that defy his humble beginnings in his new country. As the title of the memoir suggests, the hero allows himself a radical acceptance of his circumstances, which predicates his many gestures of bravery. While isolation, abandonment, poverty, and continual obstacles are familiar territory for him, and often appear to put him at the brink of annihilation—literally and emotionally—he finds a fundamental comfort and friendliness with himself, an inner companionship at the heart of his spirituality. Therefore, the physical beating heart inside him becomes a touchstone and oracle of survival—something worthy of a string of self-help books, and no doubt a source of strength for his psychiatric practice, which brings him great respect among his colleagues.

A consummate observer of the diverse cultures that comprise his adopted nation, Hong maintains throughout his life an affinity for the underclass, always sympathizing with the underdogs, dreamers, and workaday metaphysicians. We are inspired by his relentless insistence on achieving his dreams in spite of sometimes-devastating setbacks and the negligence of his own parents and guardians, and the occasional bad business deal, yet he always finds good fortune and success.

Hong's memoir reveals the nuances of the lucid immigrant eye that is so deeply connected to the soul and origin of our nation. We watch a young man's world get continually larger as he ventures into new opportunities, earns his first dollar, and directly apprehends the land and its people as a missionary and true pilgrim while revealing an uncommon sensitivity to his fellow citizens regardless of race or class. His travels in the late '50s take us from the migrant farm workers and chanting beatniks near Santa Rosa, California, to a family of a poor black barber in Louisiana who take him in and bring him to a rural dance hall for what becomes a transformative experience for the young pilgrim, as he is exposed to Southern roots rhythm and blues in a way that few Americans get the chance to experience.

This is among other things a Christian story, as Hong's faith directs him through his early years in America. Yet, we are never preached to, nor do we experience the pitfalls of dogma or predictable judgmental attitudes. On the contrary, we see a tender, ever-searching soul trying to follow the footsteps of his hero, Albert Schweitzer—and to some degree succeeding with his consistent compassion and affinity for the dispossessed, struggling and "off-centered" of the world. We also witness a young man with a great intellectual curiosity negotiating his experiences through classical literature, music, philosophy, and the rapidly emerging ideas of his time.

This is a document of historical significance that recounts the first moments of the bombardment near Seoul from the North on the infamous day of June 25, 1950, and the subsequent adjustments of the Korean people until war's end, followed by the massive rebuilding of the country by the Americans. Hong also enters America (1956) at the initiation of intense social change and intellectual upwelling. He encounters Freedom Riders and ponders the women's movement

I. DAVID HONG MD, US NAVY CAPTAIN, RETIRED

and the Kinsey Report with the rest of the nation. We also receive an authentic Korean cultural immersion in the opening chapters and upon his subsequent return to his homeland, and therein a palpable exposure to its people from the inside, including stories and folktales of the region. Given the breadth of territory that this memoir covers through his process of immigration, its cultural hybridism remains a source of both intriguing tension and appropriate resolution as a full circle is made when Hong returns to Korea to find his true soul-companion, as well as tending to the ghosts that had separated him from his father. In so doing, Hong builds a bridge between vastly different nations as a man of uncommon conscience and indomitable will, as he realizes the dream he cast forth as a child.

Chapter One

Old World Roots

I am, according to my aunt, the thirty-third first-born son of the Hong lineage, over 600 years of traceable ancestry originating from Kaseung, the capital of the old Korean Kingdom fifty miles northeast of Seoul. Beyond that, there is no family history or extant oral tradition—only names. It was from Kaseung that my grandfather came down to Seoul at the beginning of Japanese rule in Korea. My mother's family came from further north in Manchuria. The name Hong is not common in Korea, but is known as *Yang-ban*, or a "high-class" family. I suspect our origins are in China, around 700 years ago that coincides with Genghis Khan's Mogul invasion into Korea. One of Khan's ruling administrators was probably named Hong.

My grandfather, Heung-Soo Hong, was the oldest of six brothers born by two wives, all in Seoul in the 1880s. When Seoul became the new seat of the Korean Kingdom, the clan moved there with the entire court. When my grandmother married my grandfather, she entered his house on an ornate hand-carved palanquin with gold, red, and green embroidery of brilliant rare blossoms, carried on the shoulders of four men. She also had two attending house cleaners, one for the chamber and one for outside. Her family was much wealthier than my grandfather's clan who were known as scholars, but lost much of their wealth and prestige after the 1910 Japanese annexation of Korea. My grandmother's clan adapted much more easily to the new Japanese order and became wealthy businessmen, judges, and government power players.

My grandfather was a minister in the King's cabinet and had the fifth highest position in the late Korean Kingdom before Japanese colonization. His name is engraved on the monument in the old palace court, which is now a museum in

I. DAVID HONG MD, US NAVY CAPTAIN, RETIRED

the center of old Seoul where as a boy I watched on the way to school General Eisenhower's motorcade for the armistice meeting in 1952.

My father was the oldest of my grandfather's three sons and grew up near the old palace in central Seoul. He was born the same year Korea was annexed by Japan in 1910, after the Russian Imperial Navy was demolished on the Korean Strait, the origin place of the *Kamikaze*, or "divine wind." After the Japanese occupation, my grandfather lost his scholar/administrator position in the court, unwanted in the new order, and unwilling to adapt to Japanese rule.

Somehow, after high school, my father crossed illegally by himself to Japan where he worked odd jobs while living in a rooming house and working his way through school, somehow graduating from the prestigious Waseda University in Tokyo, the Japanese equivalent of Harvard. He had a great gift for language and was a bit of a chameleon, always enchanted with exotic foreign cultures. This trait would prove to be a great asset for our survival during and after the terrible civil war in Korea. After returning to Seoul during Japanese occupation, he was a marketable commodity—well educated, fluent in Japanese, and ready for the new Japanese order in Asia.

Mom and Dad were married in the early 1930s, at the apex of the Japanese-Korean Empire that spanned throughout Japan, Formosa, China, and the Philippines. Both were well educated in the Japanese establishment, working and living with the Japanese to colonize Taiwan, where my older sister, Nami, was born. There is a picture of my father and mother on a trip to Borneo and Sumatra in the early 1930s with three dark-skinned smiling natives with pierced noses, body paint, and bows and arrows. My mother is in full western dress with an alligator handbag, high heels, and a feathered hat, resembling the American roaring '20s style. She always exuded an unusual flair and independence for a Korean woman. Father was selected as an administrator for the pharmaceutical sales in Formosa and China by an American company in Korea, founded by my mother's older brother, Ilhan New.

Uncle Ilhan was brought by an American missionary from Pyongyang to Kearney, Nebraska, in 1896 when he was nine years old. He graduated from the University of Michigan and became a successful businessman in America, returning to Korea in the 1920s to set up a large pharmaceutical company now known as Yuhan Corporation. He also founded La Choy foods in America, now an enormous worldwide corporation. His companies were all tremendously successful and still are today, representing Pfizer, Chrysler, and many other American companies, with exclusive rights to marketing and distributing dozens of American products in Korea, Formosa, Manchuria, and Japan. He became a multi-millionaire in the '20s and a celebrity throughout Korea. My mother, by her attachment to him, also became a celebrity of sorts—and a renowned hospital administrator, evangelist, and philanthropist. She was fiercely ambitious, indomitable, like most of the pioneers from the rugged north of Manchuria. She graduated from the Presbyterian

Missionary Nursing School in Pyongyang and aimed for the top from the beginning, unwilling to be held back by the needs of her children or husband.

My mother, father, and I lived with my grandma, Nami, and two younger sisters, Misa and Julie, along with a maid in a Japanese-style home in central Seoul near the old palace between the ancient east and south gates to the city. There was a main building with a separate cottage with outhouse across a large driveway where father's taxis were parked nightly. In the back was an elaborate Japanese garden filled with large bonsai evergreens and black landscape rocks framing terraced walkways and a small pond that Dad designed in the 1930s. On one side of our property was a girl's high school; and on the other, across our large vegetable garden, was a residential compound of American Presbyterian missionary families, which greatly intrigued us kids.

My earliest memory is of my father, mother, and I riding a two-wheeled rickshaw pulled by a grinning driver with a sweaty red cloth wrapped around his head. This was perhaps my first time outside the gates of our property and I will never forget my excitement in seeing the people, shops, and trees whirring past as we sped through the crowded streets, pulled by a friendly, enthusiastic driver. I remember Dad leaning back and laughing, smoking his pipe with his arm around me, teaching me the features of his beloved city. Once he took me on such an excursion to a museum where I saw an enormous prehistoric-looking fish or whale that was, to my shock, about ten times bigger than him. I thought that it looked like a bear with no legs. It made me extremely curious about other life-forms and the great diversity and classifications of animals and life on the planet. I was enamored with science from then on.

Before the war, I was one of several kindergarten boys selected to visit the Korean Broadcasting Company to sing a popular Korean children's song in front of a microphone in a large studio for a live broadcast. We harmonized wonderfully and I remember, even that early, being enthralled with the act of singing and live performance, something I retained the rest of my life. The tune stayed with me for days; and I longed to sing before an audience—in either a group or solo. It was a song about a boy riding his bicycle very fast through the city streets for the first time, ringing his bell, hoping not to hit the pedestrians.

As the oldest and only son, I was given the privilege of freely pursuing my curiosities. My first obsession, just like in the song, was riding my bike furiously about town ringing my bell with glee, yelling at people to clear out as I zoomed by. The eldest sons in Korea are given much tolerance in this regard, as we were expected to become the leaders. My first name, Inpow, actually means "benevolent leader in Chinese," or something close to that. I suspect I caught on to this advantage early and milked it for all it was worth!

A bicycle at that time was a rare possession for a boy my age; and it became my obsession after Father bought, refurbished, and painted a used one for me.

I. DAVID HONG MD, US NAVY CAPTAIN, RETIRED

This was after my mother left for America followed by Aida, my other caretaker. Aida had lived with us since before I can remember, so it was double loss for me, though I barely remember them leaving. At that same time, Father also gave me a Cocker Spaniel, named "King," and who became my constant companion and would even keep up with me as I rode endlessly through the streets on my bike. My Aunt Young-Ye Lee and Uncle Young-Gak, Father's youngest brother, also moved in with us after Mother and Aida. Aunt Young-Ye started teaching numbers, raising me until I would leave Korea and me the alphabet. A younger maid moved in as well. Sadly, my mother would exist almost entirely as a somewhat mysterious woman in photographs and my father's stories, and occasional letters until she returned seven years later.

My father often entertained friends with drinks, dinners, and games of Go under his beloved gazebo, which was surrounded by the violet blossoms of the wisteria trees in the summer. He was a Japanophile ever since he graduated from Waseda and often said that Korea was much improved by the influence of the Japanese. He continually collected Japanese antiques, art, and furniture.

The house in which I was born in 1940 is still a blueprint of my reality. In the center was a large, busy kitchen connected to a larger family room where my grandmother slept with my sisters. The clay floor was covered with thick, lacquered paper and was kept warm by the always-burning kitchen oven with a chimney that heated the clay floors from below the house—the traditional Korean heating system. On another side of the kitchen was the maid's quarters, a smaller floor-heated room connected to a larger room used for rice storage and other staples. My wifeless father and I slept in another floor-heated room. Through the sliding doors was a large storage area that held heating fuel and other supplies and imperishables.

We had a four-foot tall, 200-gallon indoor hot tub where we all bathed once a week. It had a wooden seat inside and a cast-iron furnace with a mouth opening to the outside where we fed it scraps of wood for several hours to heat the tub for early evening. There was also a bench outside under a cold shower. My father and I would bathe together first, then grandma, and then all the girls took theirs together with noisy excitement. The maid bathed last.

All four kids without Mother often slept in the same room with Grandma during the cold winter nights during the Korean War when the rooms were scarcely heated to conserve fuel. We competed for the thick ceramic body warmer filled with hot water that we kept inside our blankets. The four of us, especially me, struggled on both sides of Grandma to be in the best position to hold and suck her breasts, like little pigs aching for our missing mother. I am not sure we understood the depth of our loss from her abandonment of us until we were adults.

The entrance to the house was through two heavy hardwood sliding glass doors. Inside the foyer was a ceramic floor where shoes were left or put in a cabinet near the door. Across the entrance was a shoji screen leading to a small sitting room where an old Seiko wall clock ticked loudly and rang every hour. In my father's room hung several pictures of his deceased grandfather, and a nineteenth-century German Huygens Brothers pendulum clock. There was also a western-style room covered by an antique European colonial rug. The room was originally heated by an antique French freestanding furnace that we could no longer use since the coal supply from the north was curtailed in 1945. Dad kept a hand-cranked RCA gramophone in that room. It had poor sound, but swing music and old Steven Foster songs like "Suwannee River" often played from it. My little sisters would dance an improvised Jitterbug to Dad's amusement. My father also loved all things American, and smoked highly coveted and probably illegal American Cavendish tobacco from his English briarwood pipe, a smell that I still love.

The indoor toilet was non-flushing, but we had a water faucet. The main wood corridor was insulated by glass doors facing the gazebo and wisteria trees to the west. This was the warmest spot in the house on sunny winter afternoons, and where the kids gathered to play. Underneath the carpet on the living room floor was a secret door leading to a cellar below, which we improved during the war in order to hide there and wait out the bombing raids.

The family taxis were 1940s black Dodge sedans from the Yuhan Motor Company, also owned by Uncle Ilhan's conglomerate that had exclusive rights to Chrysler in Korea. The two-man team of driver/mechanic lived in the detached cottage on our property. My father's cousin, Nampyo, was the mechanic and assistant.

Every spring, with some help, I turned over the garden patch with a shovel and planted an abundant vegetable garden with spices, tomatoes, corn, cucumbers, zucchini, and whatever other seeds I found to try. At the corner of the house was a wire walk-in cage for chickens and rabbits, which I also tended. I also raised several litters of puppies from one of my Cocker Spaniels. I loved all animals, something that has stuck with me to this day.

Nami and I would spy on the American missionary mansion next door by climbing the ladder over the tall brick fence, one our favorite forms of entertainment, and my first exposure to American culture. We would wave to them excitedly when they spotted us and continue to ogle their wares and study their customs with fascination.

The tall entrance to the family property was elaborate and secure, with a large gate for cars and a small side gate for foot traffic. It was rebuilt after an armed robbery in our home in the middle of the night by seven men when I was about seven years old, just before the war started. No one was hurt, but Dad had many valuables stolen. This was common in Seoul at the time as there were many destitute and desperately aggressive people coming down from the north to raid and rob—a foreboding introduction to far more dangerous troubles that would come from the north very soon.

Chapter Two

Motherless Years

Growing up without a mother, I slept with my father, listening to nightly legends of the Monkey King, an ancient Chinese folk tale that he read to me in Japanese until I fell asleep each night. These adventures remain in the crevices of my subconscious. The Monkey King, or Wukong, is a mythical being said to be born of a divine rock that was fertilized by the grace of heaven. He is always searching for a sacred sutra, or Buddhist teaching/scripture that holds the secrets of immortality and the wisdom of the sages of antiquity. Along the way, he meets many perils and obstacles, including treacherous demons, dragons, and evil entities. He is enigmatic, having many powers, as well as being a trickster who can transform himself into seventy-two different forms and apparitions, such as a bird, tree, or tiny insect capable of entering the bodies of great beasts and slaying them from the inside. His greatest attribute was a somersault with which he could bounce across the entire world in one leap. The Monkey King could also ride a cloud as his vehicle and travel great distances in very little time.

There was an evil emperor that was always trying to catch and slay him, but Wukong would find ever more ingenious and slippery ways to vanquish this cruel despot who aimed to destroy everything sacred, even the holy sutras. Many times the evil Emperor would appear to have Monkey King executed, but the trickster hero would always emerge unscathed, and usually more empowered than before. He is a rebel who defies the authority of earthly rulers in favor of the eternal and heavenly laws of the Buddha.

Father also told me stories about his voyage from Japan to Formosa on a steam liner. His first-class cabin bed was hung on a pole so that, whatever the movement of the boat on the rough sea; he was stabilized in a horizontal position like a compass needle. Early in the mornings, a beautiful and graceful maid in a blue kimono tiptoed into his cabin with a slightly subdued smile to see if he was awake in order to offer him early morning tea. He said she was the most beautiful woman he had ever seen and that the tea tasted heavenly in the predawn mornings of his great voyage. Father was a living, talking personal history and mythology collection for me, captivating my imagination with animated tales, customized sound effects, and great detail, always testing my memory by asking me questions as he told the stories.

During the seven years, Mother was gone when I was six years old; his beautiful stories were contradicted by heavy nightly bouts of drinking. He would come home late and loudly call after me, as I was the only one he wanted to be with. Their marriage had deteriorated well before she left. In spite of the glitter and high style of their almost noble family status, her increased demands on him took a great toll. I am sure that Father's image suffered upon her departure, but he did not interfere with her designs and ambitions. In those days, a Korean wife traveling abroad was required to have her husband's written approval, which he must have signed before she left.

He never took up with another woman; and I remained his sole, often-unwilling companion, even at his favorite drinking holes. When he was lonely, he took me to all the geisha houses, taverns, and restaurants. Once he took me to an eatery with a fifty-five-gallon iron kettle full of water and hundreds of little slimy fish that swam wildly as the fire was lit under them, and the pace of their swimming increased with the rising temperature. At a critical point, the waiter would dump a double brick of tofu into the kettle and the minnows would frantically burrow for refuge into the still cool holes of the tofu. After more time on the fire, the waiter would dig out the fish-stuffed tofu bricks, slice and serve them in a spicy soup base with fresh chopped onion—one of the most delicious things I have ever tasted.

When dad was late coming home, my grandmother would send me out to hunt him down and bring him back to the house, often leading him by his hand, or sometimes returning by taxi if he was too inebriated. I believe that this is when my caretaking sensibilities as a future doctor began to develop.

At the end of my first year in grammar school, I read a story about a girl and her younger brother who were separated from their parents during the 1945 liberation of Korea from the Japanese. During this turbulent period, many families were separated—sometimes permanently. In this case, the natural parents, who had become beggars on the streets of Seoul, died before the siblings found each other. With tears in my eyes, I read about the sister getting separated from the little boy who needed her guidance to survive. The little boy caught word of his sister's whereabouts, and that she had been adopted by a wealthy family in Seoul. He wandered the streets for days looking for her. The sister and her new family called for him all day, every day on a loudspeaker from a taxi throughout the streets of Seoul, yelling, *"Jon-Pow!"* When the younger boy, now a beggar, saw the taxi and heard his sister's voice booming on the speaker, he rushed toward her only to miss her by a few yards in the thick, confusing crowd. I agonized over this story many mornings walking to school, crying in sympathy for the young boy, reading the book in the busy alleys, unable to put it down. Perhaps it spoke to my own abandonment issues with my mother. One of the reasons I did so well in my early schooling was because of the time-spent reading that book.

I was skipped ahead to the third grade, which isolated me and made me ill at ease. By fourth grade, I came out of my shell and explored new friendships, joined the track team, and became more confident. My interest in disease and human abnormalities was evident already, as I was intrigued by a very large retarded boy in my class who slurred, drooled, and moved in awkward spasms. I studied him for weeks with curiosity and pity and one day felt compelled to prod him with my sharp American pencil. I was scared when, after I poked him, he screamed and wailed so loudly that the teacher had to interrupt class and tend to him. I was scolded in front of the class. In retrospect, I think I was just looking for a response and information so as to determine his condition, but was rather cruel, as most children can be, and felt bad about traumatizing him. I became curious about retarded people and tried to think of cures for them.

There was another strange, mumbling retarded child close to my age that lived near some cousins of ours. He was most curiously and disturbingly kept in a closet for prolonged periods and would take his meals and often sleep there. I asked why he was being punished this way, but got no satisfactory answers from his mother, or my grandma. I continued to have strange and disturbing dreams about him for weeks, wishing that there was some way I could cure him as well.

Once I was so angry with a classmate when he took my coveted American pencil; I surprised myself with my own aggression, and for the first of only three times in my life slugged someone. These pencils were hard to come by and were also a link to my mysteriously absent mother, and I suppose a part of my identity at the time, as they distinguished me from my classmates.

However, my ultimate social identity was as the eldest son of the eldest brother; therefore I was required to attend all the Hong family functions with my grandmother, always being dragged to weddings, birthdays, and funerals. Sometimes we walked long distances or rode buses for these, or occasionally took taxis, as that was better for Grandma's image—something always of concern in Korea.

Chapter Three

The Civil War: Chaos and Blood on the Streets

In the predawn hours of June 25, 1950, a loud bombardment from the north was suddenly upon us and drawing closer to Seoul by the hour in a firestorm of heavy artillery. Everything was still before a great and momentous rumbling shook all the earth and awakened the people of Seoul. When the first day of bombing stopped around noon, I snuck out of the house and went down the deserted street. The streetcars had stopped; and about two blocks away was a huge Russian-built North Korean tank, fully armed and moving slowly to the center of town. This was one of 242 that were then invading south of the thirty-eighth parallel. I explored further on foot, up another block to the intersection of the old palace. There was a truck on fire around the corner and the smell of leaking gasoline and spent shells. Some shells from the burning truck exploded, igniting the gasoline and causing another loud explosion, sending me running home scared. Within days, the electricity and telephones were dead. Fighter planes and bombers were on the assault, and supply infrastructure was being laid by the Communist forces for a long campaign that would change our family and nation forever.

On June 26, my father told me that he needed to go to the other side of town, about a two-hour walk, to see if his deceased brother's family was all right. My father had two younger brothers, the youngest of which moved into our home with his wife when my mother left. They did not have any children. The other brother, an accountant, died in our home of typhus spread by body lice in 1945 after he returned from a Japanese mining operation in North Korea. I remember seeing him get weaker and thinner every day with IVs in his arm, all pale and wan. He was treated by a doctor, but there were no antibiotics in Korea in 1945.

I. DAVID HONG MD, US NAVY CAPTAIN, RETIRED

At the age of forty, Father could not walk through the newly occupied streets without significant risk; but with a small child in tow, he would be safe from being mistaken as a combatant. Hand-in-hand we went through the narrow alleyways to avoid the Communist Korean soldiers, occasionally passing them though the open streets. In an unusual way, I was able to protect him with my innocence while he protected me as a father. We finally arrived at his brother's house, relieved to see my aunt and three cousins in tact, but very frightened, as we all were.

A week or so later, American bombers started flying in continuous intervals above us in broad daylight. I sat on the fence, looking down on the city below and watched the aerial shows. A formation of four high-speed propeller-driven bombers appeared at noon and, one by one, dove almost to the ground and fired rockets toward the railroad station creating enormous explosions followed by huge black billows of smoke rising high in the clear summer sky. These bombings from an aircraft carrier near Inchon continued almost daily for weeks. A few weeks later they were being met by Russian-built anti-aircraft shells bursting in the air from Communist ground forces. As I recall, they never hit a single American plane. During this battle, armed North Korean soldiers were coming into the neighborhoods, harassing, and looting from civilians. Several came to our house and drove away in our taxi, asking if we had another hidden somewhere on the grounds. Luckily, we were able to keep the second. One tall soldier with a pockmarked face surprised me by asking in a kind and gentle tone where my mother was. I was afraid and told him she was dead.

Food soon became scarce in the summer of 1950. Almost 99% of Seoul's population was trapped and powerless, unable to escape into the countryside since the Han River Bridge was destroyed by retreating South Korean forces. All we had to eat at our place were the garden vegetables I had planted. Some North Korean soldiers, mostly officers, had moved into the missionary complex next door. After about a month, my sister and I gathered the courage to put the ladder up and peek over the brick fence to see what they were doing. We waved at them enthusiastically as they ate over an open fire in the yard. They waved back and smiled and from then on, we made a daily ritual of climbing up to spy on them as they ate, laughed, and shot targets with their pistols. One day when it dawned on them that we were, just hungry kids watching them eat out of an enormous stew pot full of meat and vegetables. Acutely feeling our hunger, we waved more vigorously. After supper, two officers in crisp, clean uniforms came toward our wall with a twenty-gallon drum of stew, put it on our side of the fence and went back without saying a word. We were elated and ate well for nearly a month from that allotment, starting with an almost celebratory feast the first night, inviting all our relatives to feast on the meat which none of us had tasted in two months.

Before long we were all starving for protein again, having consumed all of our chickens a long time ago, and even the vegetable yield was thinning due to a hot summer. One day late in the summer, my father wanted to go to the Han River for fish. We started out early in the morning and walked for over eight hours. We spent the first night at a friend's house, and early the next morning went down to the river to find an available boat. We found a fisherman that had just caught a great many eels, my father's favorite food, and soon to be mine. While he was negotiating for the eels, we heard bombs bursting a few miles up river near the old Han River railroad bridge, built by the Japanese in the early 1920s. In the sky, I could see tiny mirror-like reflections of moving planes, barely visible to the naked eye. They were bombing the bridge again to impede Communist supply lines. The Communists were constantly repairing the bridge, and the Americans were destroying it. I sat transfixed for an hour watching the explosions. Father told me that these B-29s were larger than our house, with crews of five men, each equipped with a parachute in case the plane was hit, and that they could fly thousands of miles. If the planes landed on water, they had inflatable boats with all sorts of water and fishing gear and built-in radios to signal their position. I became fascinated with the advanced and mighty engineering of the Americans. For a young boy in Korea, it seemed as if Americans had magical powers, able to defy limitations the rest of us had. That is when I got my first notion of visiting America.

By September 1950, there was increased intensity in the bombardments as the Americans reoccupied the South and neared in on recapturing Seoul. Father and I started digging beneath the foundation of the house to make a secret hideaway below the western room. We brought in lumber and anything else we could find: metal sheets, bedsprings, and poles for reinforcement to put under the ceiling to cushion the impact of a large shell, should it hit. We spent several days doing this until all was quiet. As it turned out, only one errant shell landed in Seoul, leaving a gaping hole in a house two blocks away. Luckily, no civilians were hurt in that particular campaign, as the Americans were careful and knew the area was crammed with innocent people. They were hitting the then-retreating Communist targets to the north.

In early September, the bombardment completely stopped and an eerie silence set in as we waited, trying to determine if it was safe to go out to try to get food again. We came out of our bunker and Dad suggested we check on his brother's family once again. We left our house and entered the alleyways out to the main street toward the East Gate, one of the most famous landmarks of old Seoul, even today, as it represents the center of the old Chosun Kingdom. The South Gate was also significant with its famous classic Western-style railroad station, built in 1910 by the Japanese as a memorial to *Pax Sinica* in Asia. These two gates, along with the north and west gates in the more remote mountain areas were the only entrances to the capital of the old kingdom.

I. DAVID HONG MD, US NAVY CAPTAIN, RETIRED

When we arrived at the East Gate, the city was deserted; and there was heavy fortification with three tiers of machine guns manning the crossroads through which all supplies and soldiers had to pass, as well as all the traffic in and out of the area, as it was the main hub of Seoul. As we were about to turn the corner of the intersection, a lone American jeep with a trailer and only one soldier in it was moving increasingly fast, maybe 60 or 70 mph toward the gate. It passed us in a great cloud of dust, and a group of North Korean soldiers yelled "Yankee! Yankee!" and shot hundreds of rounds at the speeding jeep in just a few seconds from several locations. Some of the bullets ricocheted near us, and I was not even sure I was alive until I heard my father calling after me. When I looked back, the jeep was gone, appearing to have made it through. We continued walking carefully hand-in-hand across the street to the other side, passing several dead and bleeding bodies that apparently were there before the gunfire. I remember being surprised at the sheer volume of blackish blood that gathered in pools down a small incline of the street. To this day, I wonder if the American made it through safely. I suspect he may have been lost and trapped behind enemy lines and deliberately braved that gauntlet as his best chance at remaining uncaptured. We continued cautiously toward my aunt's house.

For all my father's deficiencies, he kept a strong sense of responsibility and displayed continual courage in looking after the extended family in those difficult times. He would engage North Korean soldiers occasionally to get information and other resources, even though there was risk of violence. He seemed to command respect, even from the often hostile and irrational young Communist troops. At forty, he was considered an elder by the young troops, was usually respected, and utilized this to assist our family's survival through this period of chaos and famine. However, once a young South Korean soldier hit him in the face very hard with the butt of his rifle when he engaged him in conversation. It was completely unprovoked.

These were chaotic and confusing times during which the people were unusually desperate and irrational. We had to remain constantly aware and suspicious of almost everybody in our midst. During these weeks and months, I learned, perhaps at too early an age, how to survive in a brutal world. No one was prepared for this harsh reality, regardless of age or class; and I was fortunate to have a protective father that avoided the draft into the military, or surely, I would have been a lost orphan in Korea, like the brother and sister from the story I knew so well.

Chapter Four

Survival Is Victory

By October 1950, the Chinese were crossing into the Yale River into North Korea en masse. We heard the news loudly and clearly through the radio and newspaper that Seoul was soon to evacuate. By early November, the entire city was being vacated as the government asked everyone to move south. However, in our case, my grandmother and sisters, who were only five and seven years old, would not be able to endure the cold winter walking. My aunt and uncle offered to take Nami, the oldest at eleven, with them as a refugee to Nonsan, about fifty miles south of Osan Air Force Base. The fever to evacuate intensified as the Communist Chinese were only thirty miles north of us; and the Americans had pulled out—and there were few signs of South Korean soldiers. Only a few percent of the population, mostly the elderly and infirmed, stayed in the city. We could tell by the relatively few fires that burned in the cold winter mornings.

In the frenzy of the evacuation, my father and I ventured outside to buy rice and other staples for the long winter ahead. Even in our bare bones necessity situation, Dad, ever the antique collector, found a large stone pagoda that he could not resist and found a way to bring this 2000-pound relic home in three pieces. He and several laborers delivered and set it up inside the gate of our property over the course of an entire day.

The entrance of the Maoist "volunteer" army was very eerie. There was no noise or gun fighting—in fact, it was totally silent. One day I heard something rumbling on the street and ran down to the alley to peek, seeing only one moving truck and a few soldiers on foot. I came home the next day to explore and saw a large traditional Korean household about a block away where my good friend used to live. I peeked inside, sure that he had left, and saw about twenty Chinese soldiers eating and relaxing. When I asked for my friend, an interpreter came out and said simply, "He does not live here now." I saw only rifles and cooking utensils in the house, and many of the soldiers were disguised in civilian clothes.

Because of the nightly aerial surveillance and occasional bombing, we put up heavy black curtains all around the windows to avoid detection from above. Still, we had to light kerosene lamps inside to function. One night a tremendous bursting bomb came very close to our house. We were glad to be alive, and upon peeking through the curtain saw the entire sky light up. We opened a window and went outside across the taxi driveway beyond the brick wall to the other side of the property to see the missionary vegetable garden was on fire with oily, stinky flames rising a hundred feet into the air, creating so much heat we could not stay outside. We were afraid our house might burn down as well, but the brick wall was thick and high enough to keep the fire and liquid fuel at bay. Later I learned that this was a napalm bomb, and it would not be the last.

By February 1951, we were again running out of food. I was now ten years old and considerably stronger than the previous year, and could venture out on foot with Father for a three-day foraging walk to a remote farming village where distant relatives lived. Early one cold morning, we started out with three days of supplies on our backs toward the familiar Han River Bridge where I had seen the B29s in action, and where we had found the eels to bring home only six months ago. We arrived at the house we had stayed at on the previous trip to find it empty, along with an entirely abandoned village. We did our best to secure a night's stay in the empty house and started a fire in the kitchen. There was a well that was frozen over, but with some difficulty, we drew some ice out to boil.

The next morning at daybreak, the coldest part of the day, we walked across the frozen river with my dog, King, who my father insisted we bring to alert us of potential danger along the way, and also show Communist soldiers that we were locals. On shore, we saw a tall structure that housed a steel cable that crossed the river, and many large shells and open, stacked ammunition boxes scattered about. There were no soldiers to be seen. Scared to death and holding hands with King following us, we walked two hundred yards into the middle of the Han River, avoiding the steel cable. We finally saw a soldier who yelled at us to stop, motioning for us to come toward him. Noticing that he was Chinese, my father spoke fluently in his language, causing the soldier to lighten up, and he asked us some questions. We replied that we were simply on our way to the country to get food for my grandmother and younger sisters. The lone sentry unbuttoned his heavily braided gray cotton coat, put his hand in his chest pocket, and pulled out an unlabeled can and gave it to us with a smile before letting us pass. I suspect it was his ration for the day. Father told me that this was a common humanitarian gesture among the Chinese, especially in rural areas. He also reminded me that the same degree of kindness was rarely seen among our harsh, authoritarian compatriot soldiers. A similar situation is what got him the rifle butt to the head by a young Korean soldier near our home six months earlier.

In the middle of the river as the sun rose, we could see large open holes in the ice from the previous day's bombing, with several scattered and frozen dead bodies. I could not tell if they were civilians or soldiers, but they were all men. Quickly and carefully, we moved from the danger to the other side of the river where we rested and ate lunch under a clear sunny sky and then proceeded toward Kimpo Air Force Base.

On our way to Kimpo, we crossed a well-traveled automobile bridge over a tributary of the Han River. It was the only bridge to Kimpo, and I had crossed it many times by bus. This was about twenty miles from the farmhouse where my aunt was raised—our destination for the night. Her family had a large rice farm at the foothills of the Mountains. My aunt used to take me to her mother's place there for a month every year. It was a treat for me to fish in the country, gather persimmons and other vegetables, and go clamming at the shores of the river. We gathered chestnuts there in the fall, and it seemed to be a land of infinite bounty. We approached the bridge, which was about eighty yards long and twelve feet wide, and bare except for two parallel steel frames, probably intentionally stripped, about twenty yards above the frozen river.

We had two options. We could either walk on the steel bars, or cross the treacherous ravine below, which would require a long roundabout detour. Father decided we could walk the steel bars carefully and started ahead of me as I followed. King was hesitant. I called him repeatedly; and he came a step or two, then only to retreat. We had to proceed without him if necessary. King then decided to go down across the ravine. We were almost to the other side of the bridge when I heard him howling loudly from below as we increased our distance from him. I did not look back or below as I followed the steel beam with all my concentration to the end. When I had crossed to the shore below, I looked back and King was still running back and forth at the frozen river's edge. I called him across the ice and finally coaxed him into crossing. He pounced forth in nervous jerky movements, approached the small hole near the middle of the river (where someone fell into shortly before we arrive), and suddenly disappeared into the freezing water. I panicked as he paddled and thrashed around in the open hole, unable to get out. After a few minutes, he slowed down and was probably suffering from hypothermia. I could not stand it and decided to go out on the ice to get him. My father agreed; and I crawled on my belly toward the break in the ice, distributing my weight evenly with my belt tied around my ankle, which was attached to Dad's belt—he too crawling on his belly, holding the belt taut so he could pull me back if the ice cracked. I finally reached King's collar and pulled him gently out of the water as my father pulled me toward land.

I. DAVID HONG MD, US NAVY CAPTAIN, RETIRED

We needed to rest after this harrowing drama; and the cold, dark night was fast approaching. We knew we could not make it to the old house as we had planned and hadn't seen a living body, except the Communist soldier in the morning; but we knew there were farmers still living in the area. We took a small dirt road to a village hoping to find a farmhouse for the night. Father saw smoke from a chimney in the distance. We approached them, and he negotiated a place to eat and sleep for a small amount of money. We were famished and devoured whatever the host had prepared. We had traveled this road many times, but things were remarkably different now. Father gave the names of the people he knew in the area to assure them he was a local. The farmer recognized one of the names and became instantly more at ease. In a few hours, they were quite friendly, even joking; and we were all enjoying the good company, a small repose from the suffering we would all endured the past several months. They discussed the war and the latest news of military maneuvers near the village. Many people were literally living underground, including adults trying to avoid forced military service at the hands of the Communists. The farmer finally confided to my father that an American pilot had been shot down near the Han River Bridge. He parachuted into the hills nearby and was being sheltered in various villages, as they moved him from place to place to help him avoid being captured. I prayed that night that the pilot was alive and safe.

The next day, we started out to my aunt's childhood home; but it was too far for me to walk, as the ground was snow covered, especially on the roadsides. We pressed on past Kimpo AFB and finally reached the house after dark and immediately heard a loud bang. There were constant spotter planes patrolling near the airport, but we never paid much attention to them until we heard that noise. Suddenly night turned into bright day for the next forty minutes amid countless explosions. We could see everything in the distance, which helped us find the road and move forward. I suspected the planes were looking for a larger target, perhaps a group of people moving across the terrain. The farmhouse turned out to be empty, as we had feared. All the furniture and equipment was gone; and to my surprise, the kitchen had been rendered unusable as the iron-cooking kettle was full of human excrement, some sort of animal marking?

The next day, we started out before dawn with little food including uncooked rice to cross the long uninhabited mountain range, over five miles wide. How pitiful we were—a near-starving man and his ten-year-old son, walking hand in hand through harsh country, desperate for even a clue as to where we might find nourishment, ever wary of armed soldiers and flying bombs. After an hour on the road, we were still climbing at an increasingly steeper grade through the isolated area. Father told me that this road was famous for armed robbers in the old days, as there was no surveillance. I thought even then at how innocuous the armed robbers were compared to the deadly Communist soldiers and weapons of destruction that were upon us now. I then saw someone suspicious coming toward us and braced for an encounter; but luckily, he crossed to the other side of the road, as he too might have been fearful of us.

As we hiked, as if I needed such stimulation, my father, always trying to entertain me, told me scary tales of evil backwoods elves; but it became too real when he told me of an elf disguised as an egg that would roll down a hillside and transform into a terrifying goblin. I got goose pimples and started conjuring thoughts of the Monkey King intervening to save us, and would beg for a Monkey King tale to counter the trauma. Father, as always, obliged and told me another tale.

We hurried toward the top of the range to exit the seemingly evil woods, passing several travelers on the way up, including one that was yelling like a psychotic, probably as a defense mechanism so that we would not engage him; or perhaps he was truly psychotic, as these trying times were pushing everyone over the edge. Finally, in the distance at the top of the mountain, we saw the glint of dawn signaling the end of the most precarious section of our journey. By late afternoon, we arrived at a remote farming village a few miles from the thirty-eighth parallel about forty miles northwest of Seoul, where I had plenty of distant relatives. An old lady greeted us, recognizing me immediately with a big, warm embrace, though I did not remember her. We spent two nights there while we negotiated a price for a large quantity of rice. The place had a straw roof, papered clay walls, and clay floors covered with lacquered paper with the traditional Korean chimney under the house to heat the floor. They had no kerosene—only candles, and very primitive tools around the farm.

In this area, food was plentiful and inexpensive and the people were friendly and simple. After two nights of wonderful rest, we left with a rickshaw full of rice and other staples on our backs. We headed back on the same mountain route, but this time it was much more difficult as we were burdened with heavy loads down the steep slopes. We rested often, but my hands were getting very cold from restriction of blood circulation from heavy load, even though I was sweating from the workout. I had to stop several times to get circulation into my arms and hands again. Father kept telling me along how proud of me he was and that I was becoming even a better young man than he had hoped. This praise sustained me, as I am sure it was meant to do through some stretches of the trail that I feared I could not endure. I never complained during the entire journey. We had to stop at the defiled house one more time, and often ate on the move to hasten our return to get this nourishment to my grandma and sisters.

The next day was sunny and very cold. We were approached from behind by a group of Chinese soldiers, white sheets dangling on their backs as they walked to the Kimpo airport toward Seoul. They had passed us by about a city block when suddenly there was a roar of four jet planes, which we had never seen or

I. DAVID HONG MD, US NAVY CAPTAIN, RETIRED

heard before. These F-86 Saber fighters were fast and completely different in their movement and patterns, leaving enormous smoke trails. They were within sight as soon as we heard them. One made a turn and dove toward us, followed by the others in formation. When they heard the roar of the fighters, the soldiers suddenly dispersed on both sides of the road, half on one side, half on the other, all covering themselves with white bed sheets. Father said we should get in the middle of the road and hold our hands high together so they could see us. As they descended to just above the road, they strafed both sides of us with machine guns; and we remained surprisingly unscathed. We were too scared to see if the Chinese had been killed, but they were all immobile on the roadsides. We rushed to pass them quickly and got home safely with a month's supply of rice and other food.

During the following months, we nearly starved as we scrounged everywhere for food, not knowing when the Americans would come back and restore normal commerce in the city. One morning Father asked that the girls be kept in the house with Grandma for a while. He told me to come outside, saying that we had to do something very difficult before we were too weak from malnutrition to take care of ourselves. He somberly proceeded to attach a rope around King's collar and looped it over a tall tree branch, then pulled the rope until the dog was hanging in the air. I watched, speechless and shocked, aware of what was going to happen, and tearfully went inside. I came out a few minutes later expecting to see his limp, dead body, and was surprised that he was still hanging and alive. In fact, when he saw me, his tail began to wag, though he was breathing laboriously and gagging. Dad saw this too, and ended the dog's suffering by drawing him down and breaking his neck with a broomstick, before hoisting him up again. He then gathered dry branches and started a fire. I watched calmly, tears rolling down my face, remembering when I had received King as a puppy and a parting gift upon Mother's departure several years earlier. Neither King nor I made a noise during this ordeal, and soon Dad was carving up the hairless carcass and set it to boiling overnight. Grandma served the soup the next day, telling the girls that we had found a pig. GIVING WAS RECEIVING. Nobody asked questions as we ate the meat for some weeks and then boiled the bones repeatedly; helping us, stay alive until the spring when US forces reoccupied Seoul.

Chapter Five

The Search for Corned Beef and the Return of Peace

Within a year, there was another UN retreat from Seoul at which time Grandma, Misa, and Julie, who were unable to walk, stayed at home with much more food to last for six months. Father, Nami, and my aunt and uncle, along with thousands of other civilian refugees departed on foot for Ansan near the present Osan AFB, sixty miles southeast of the city over the picturesque mountain ranges. The following three weeks of walking through the countryside were among the most interesting and educational of my life. Father, a pharmacist, filled my backpack with medicines from home and carried a great amount on his back, intending to be a traveling doctor, knowing that he would encounter people in great hardship. He also knew he could barter the drugs for food, lodging, and other essentials—a very smart move. Along the way, we found a makeshift black market near the American encampments through which essential commodities flowed abundantly; probably in exchange for the sexual services of the young Korean girls we saw milling about the bustling camp. Tasty military canned meat commanded the highest price. My father could read English and was able to find the good stuff—bacon and other meat. I remember the first time I tasted bacon—it was sublime! I talked about it for weeks, and craved that flavor in my dreams. Sometimes we would manage to get a gallon of butter, which was overpriced and disappointing the first time when my sisters and I tried to eat it from the can. Not everything heavy was meat.

Eventually we arrived at a small remote hideaway village at the foothills of a small mountain where we rented two rooms in a farmer's house. My uncle, aunt, and sister slept in one room, while Father and I slept in the other. By this time, Father and Uncle, both being under forty-five, were targets for martial conscription as laborers to carry ammunition to the front line in the mountains. We had not seen a policeman for months, until around two o'clock that morning when there was a loud knock at our door, which woke us with a startle. Father, who was sleeping nude, as did I to lessen the bites of the army fleas, bolted out of the window with a crash and ran behind the wooden fence and disappeared into the darkness toward the foot of the mountain. I remember seeing him reach to the ground to pick up a piece of stray canvass to cover himself as he ran surprisingly fast for a forty-three-year-old man! If dire danger were not so imminent, it would have been funny how he held the canvass around his privates as he tried to run at top speed. Thereafter, we vigilantly changed our sleeping quarters every few days among different families in the village who generously supported our need to evade the police and keep our relative freedom. Later we heard that the death rate for draftees on the supply and ammunition lines was 75%.

Five miles from where we were staying in Ansung, there was a large American army construction company which displayed amazing machinery, including a tall steam hammer that drove huge telephone posts deep into the riverbed to enlarge the older, weaker bridge to accommodate tank transporters and other military movement. Wherever Americans went, village life was good with an ever-flowing supply of conveniences, tools, and most importantly, food. Even the garbage dump was filled with waxed cardboard boxes, which were a bonanza of building materials for displaced families to use as temporary sidewalls in the monsoon season. There was a sprawling black market with beds, blankets, and leftover table food, which was highly prized to help us raise pigs. One day Nami and I went shopping in the black market looking for cans of corned beef or whatever else we could find. Father was acting as village doctor, administering medicines and trading drugs for food and other supplies. Neither my sister nor I knew English; but we eventually became well trained at identifying English characters on the cans that indicated the best products, whereas before, we would simply have to guess and open the cans to see if we had corned beef and hash or stewed tomatoes. It was a crapshoot until we got more experience. We studied English characters very carefully so we could find what we liked on the black market. The soldiers also would trade or simply give us sundries and creature comforts, such as insecticide to ward off the fleas, our arch enemy, perhaps even more troubling than the Communist forces.

We arrived after a hot, sweaty, five-mile walk and asked around for canned corned beef; but the sellers were often devious and misleading as to what was in the cans, as most customers knew even less English than us and were playing the same lottery game with regard to contents. We concentrated on the solid, heavy cans, which indicated beef, hopefully not butter! We also got adept at shaking the contents to determine the likelihood of it being meat. We did not want fruit, as much better fresh fruit was still available in the countryside during the summer. Sometimes there were open cans of beef left over from prospective buyers who could not pay after they somehow got the sellers to open the cans. These were available for much less. Once we brought home a very dense can that when we opened, it contained a thick, oily substance we had never seen, which turned out to be peanut butter. It tasted good the first couple of days combined with rice and vegetables; but after eating it three times a day for a week, we grew tired of it, to where it hurt our stomachs to smell the stuff! We studied the characters, to make sure not to buy it again. We were always after the elusive corned beef! A college student and distant relative, also hiding from military conscription, showed me more of the alphabet and how to decipher words like "meat" and how to pronounce them, essentially learning alphabet. I became highly motivated and quickly memorized dozens of food words, and soon was able to hit the bull's eye every time.

In the same village across from the house where we were staying lived a grotesquely disfigured, solitary woman that we would see at the common well twice a day. Everybody avoided her because she had what father explained to me was the incurable disease of leprosy. The discovery of a treatment for this disease was a curiosity to me for long after. He told me, as Korean parents customarily told children to keep them away from the diseased ones, that lepers were evil and liked to cut open little kids' bellies and eat their livers to cure their disease. Even as a young child, I constantly thought of diseases, symptoms, and potential cures for the people around me and spent a great deal of time trying to reason through the problem of the idea of "incurable"—something I had a hard time accepting.

Near the Ansung River, my father decided to fish at a good-sized lake that filled up nicely after the monsoon rains. Fresh fish was still our favorite food, and we were even getting tired of canned American beef. There was a series of running streams emptying into the lake and dozens of refugees fishing. We spotted many large fish in a larger lake nearby, some over a foot long; but it was inaccessible as we had no boat or other necessary equipment to get to the deeper water where the big fish stay during the hot hours of the day. We used a mosquito net to catch a lot of minnows and other small fish, but were not excited about those, as they were more for bait than eating. Luckily, an American army truck stopped nearby to watch us while resting. My father approached the soldiers, speaking his best English; and they responded gregariously, surprised to hear a Korean speaking their language somewhat fluently. Father requested on behalf of all the residents of the village that the GIs throw one of the grenades from their belts into the lake. We were so hungry for the taste of fish! The two young soldiers laughed at the idea, but understood how hungry the village was, and perhaps they were a little bored too—so they obliged with a good sense of humor, giggled to each other, and told us all to clear out for a while. A soldier then threw in a single grenade; and in an enormous blast, almost like a volcano, a funnel of water shot up from the lake with hundreds of stunned, freshly killed fish—a veritable bonanza, more than enough for all the villagers to stuff into their baskets. Even minutes after the blast, fish continued to funnel toward the top of the water as people came back for second and third loads in a mad and joyous scene. The entire village had a jubilant feast that night as all the stoves and outdoor fires roasted fresh fish. Seeing was believing.

By early fall, all was peaceful again; and we were allowed to return to Seoul en masse to rebuild our lives. US forces continued to rebuild major infrastructure, including large pontoon bridges across the Han River at two different points and paving the bomb-decimated roads, as well as making entirely new ones. I saw for the first time and was amazed by the mighty US construction machinery, which I would watch with fascination for hours as the city was rebuilt before my eyes. Buses converted from army trucks served as our mass transport system and brought people from as far as Pusan, over 200 miles away. The population increased threefold in a matter of months, mostly from country refugees resettling in Seoul from decimated farms, as most had no young men to work them because the death toll was beyond anyone's imagination. Soon there were new electric American streetcars—twice as many as we had before. Every imaginable tool flooded into the black market along the famous huge open sewer canal that ran through the center of town, lined with thousands of shacks on both sides.

Now that Seoul was teaming with life again, father opened a pharmacy near our home in the oldest and busiest part of Seoul on Chong-Roe Street, half a mile west of the East Gate. Reconstruction was happening everywhere as donated materials flooded in, including the nearby Seoul University hospital, occupied by the US Army.

Soon it was time to go back to school, and I found I was skipped over fifth grade to sixth and became the Science Chairman for my class of about ninety. I became obsessed with science and electricity, learning how radios worked, and eventually making my own with a magnet and battery with surplus earphone. I also made my own small electric motor, using a tin can with a magnet into motion. I didn't know anything about Benjamin Franklin's dangerous experiments with electricity and flying kites in storms, but figured out how to tap electricity by running a copper wire cable that I found in our yard parallel to a high voltage electricity line, which created a continuous magnetic field and free electricity to light automobile headlights in my room. Later, I created a primitive rheostat for my radio, blissfully unaware how dangerous it was.

There was a direct streetcar line between Father's drug store and my school; so after school, I would disembark and help him by taking home the day's cash safely in my school bag, as street robberies were rampant, and shop owners leaving their stores at the end of the business day were prime targets.

At the end of sixth grade, a nationwide test was given wherein the first top 200 scorers would be selected to attend a special advanced junior high school, the next highest 200 scores would go to Seoul Junior High School, and the last 200 in the nation would go to the least prestigious school in the nation. Every school was funded by a combination of government subsidies, private tuition. Large donations prompted admission better schools regardless student's score in this national testing. I made it to the top second school; and my academic career was about to take off with real purpose, as I aimed to be an architect to help rebuild Seoul.

It turns out that the son of the South Korean vice president was in my class too, as well as the son of the Secretary of Education, no doubt with money and political power. The vice president's son was an enigma to me, as he flaunted his status and money by driving his own jeep to school when no one else had their own transportation, and riding around on his own horse—something I had always dreamed of, but would likely never have. He also brought his .45 pistol to school and constantly showed it off, immune to any discipline from the school faculty. A few years later, he made national news as he killed both his father and himself with that same pistol during the first Korean popular uprising against S. M. Rhee.

I now could ride the buses and streetcars as I pleased, something that I have always loved—watching the city and its people go by, taking in the smells and sounds of different parts of Seoul. Sometimes I took the hour walk to school with friends, checking out the shops, candy stores, and magazines along the way. I walked so much and grew so fast that Father could not keep me in shoes. He finally talked me into getting a pair of army combat boots resized to fit me. The heels started to wear unevenly, so I taught myself how to walk with more balance and equal distribution of weight on each foot and made the boots last two years.

Once while at home carrying a heavy piece of sheet metal the ersatz ping-pong table with my neighbor, I slipped and dropped it on my foot, slicing it open. It proceeded to swell and get infected although I cleaned with soap and water in the subsequent days. Father was irritable and drunk much of that period of time, so I decided to give myself penicillin shot. I boiled the syringe and needle, carefully inserted the needle into the rubber top after cleaning with alcohol, and slowly inserted the needle into the area on my buttock after cleaning thoroughly with alcohol as I had seen father do many times. I never told my father about this, as he would likely have punished me. The swelling and infection subsided over the next two days, and I felt a great sense of pride in having treated myself. In retrospect, this was a pivotal moment in my path to becoming a doctor. I had an exhilarating feeling of independence and envisioned myself administering medicines to the sick and suffering and relieving their pain. There was still a great amount of suffering in Korea. I suppose that is part of the reason my mother decided to return to Korea to work in the hospital as a nurse and administrator. She also had unfinished business with her family, and no doubt had reached some conclusions as to how to proceed into the future and what was best for her children—though I still cannot fathom her reasoning.

Chapter Six

My Mother Returns After Seven Years

Mother had written Dad about three times a year, often including passages from the Bible to address his sense of loss or anger that he no doubt had communicated to her at some point. I do not think he ever wrote her back; but once he bought an expensive turn-of-the century hardwood-shipping crate and filled it with the sun-cured caviar that she loved, some of which he and I prepared together. I think he was trying to tell her he wanted her to come home and return to being a traditional family, but this was not my mother's way.

During those seven years, he was alone; he took me around, even late at night to all his favorite bars and restaurants, but never socialized with women in front of me, though there were many pretty women that approached him, as he had a good social position. One thing mother made clear in her last letter (which I read, as I read all their letters) was that she would not return as his wife. Within a month of his receiving that letter, a tall, thin very quiet woman he met through a neighbor unceremoniously moved into our house with scarcely an introduction. Initially I thought she was a housekeeper, but I finally saw her going into his bedroom at night. She was ordinary and illiterate, quite the opposite of my mother. I never understood why he settled for a woman like that.

I had received a few letters a year from my mother along with an occasional pair of American tennis shoes, a very hot commodity in Korea and much better than Korean shoes. The American pencils and ballpoint pens she sent were also much sought after. When I was twelve, father received a letter that she was returning back to Korea, but not to him! I was thirteen by the time she arrived at Pusan Harbor. Her youngest brother, Tuk-Han, invited me to greet her. We rode on a first class train; the first time for me, then took a taxi to the ship. She stood on the deck in her customary dignified style, in an expensive blue wool coat and matching scarf, with every hair in place and small, detailed gold cross on a chain around her neck. I boarded the ship, and she hugged me very hard and took me to her cabin. I remembered very little of her, yet she was always in my mind, yet at the same time a source of sorrow for my father. I was glad she had returned. I was taken around the ship and given fresh sliced Florida oranges, an absolute rarity in Korea—which I happily devoured.

She brought a big American Ford sedan on the ship to use in Korea. This was impressive move as there were few taxis or limousines anymore in Korea, and all automobiles were made from converted army trucks and jeeps. Hers was luxuriously streamlined with thick carpet and leather seats and the most comfortable ride I would ever felt. She went to work right away as head of the nursing department at the Seventh Day Adventist Mission Hospital ten miles outside of Seoul.

Originally a sanitarium, it was rebuilt as a fully equipped medical facility with incoming American supplies. Mother had the best room in the nursing department, and I would see her about two days a month, sometimes sneaking up to sleep with her in her room, as no men were permitted. She would special order sweet tender American corn for us for supper—her favorite. She became quite a powerhouse in that hospital. Sometimes her luxury sedan would pick us up, and we would go to the American embassy and other important places in grand style in what was probably the only limousine in town except for the President's. One day I talked her into letting me drive it on the high school soccer field. She was surprised, yet somewhat delighted with how I drove, kicking up grass and mud.

She would end up leaving the hospital within two years to build a house in the countryside near her brother's mansion on the other side of Seoul on half way to Inchon, where the US Marines landed in 1950. Thereafter I lived half the time with her and half with Dad. I bought a bicycle one day and rode twenty miles from her place through the busy streets to school. I also liked to hitchhike, as there were many US army vehicles running between Inchon and Seoul. While I enjoyed visiting Mother's place, the tension between her and Father was quite taxing on me.

Shortly after Mother's return, she came to the house in a big truck with a driver while Dad was away and took the most valuable antique furniture and other expensive things from the house. I assume he agreed to this. The best things were gone, many of which Dad and I had picked up cruising the back roads over the years. He never complained or put up a fight. The constant antagonism between them made me frequently sick in the stomach as he continued to come home late, drunk, and grumpy, demanding my attention; but I knew I could not supply what he was missing. He was a deeply wounded man, showing no signs of renewal, and in some respects never recovered.

He continued to run his drugstore in the heart of town, specializing in American antibiotics like Teramyacin, and did well. These drugs were saving many lives and stopping infectious illnesses. Penicillin was more common and cheaper, while Teramyacin was funneled illegally into the market through an American source, as Korea was too poor to import much after the war. Dad bought many different high-priced drugs from American soldiers, taking advantage of his fluent English to get the edge on his competitors.

It was somewhere around this time that he sat me down to talk about women and family and all the father-to-son wisdom in the ways of entering manhood. He said, "All you need is a Japanese wife, American house, and a Chinese cook to have a happy life." It was hard not to ignore that he was forsaking Korean women in this formula, which surprised me; but after his experience, I can hardly blame him. I often thought he would have been better off moving to Japan and working and remarrying there.

An ongoing source of pain for all of us was their bickering over who was going to pay for the kids' tuition, clothes, and other expenses. Sometimes my father would physically push her out of his pharmacy in frustration right in front of me. She would dash to her waiting sedan and disappear. She had become extremely wealthy with almost unlimited access to American dollars through Uncle Ilhan. However, in the end Father paid the majority of my expenses; and I can scarcely remember her ever giving me even a little spending money.

One day he sent me to deliver two dozen original Yuhan Inc. stock certificates to Uncle Ilhan in exchange for his making arrangements for my sister Misa to go to America. After all these years, I cannot understand why my father was forced to exchange his few financial assets to do this for me, when my mother and uncle had such vast financial resources. The stocks, no doubt, were transferred to my mother's name. Uncle Ilhan then adopted my younger sister, Misa, but was afraid to adopt me because it might have entitled me to his inheritance. Ironically, we would both end up in American orphanages and completely disinherited. In the end, Ilhan and my mother reneged on their end of the deal; and my father ended up empty-handed with no more comfort as to his children's security. All my father's assets became my mother's, and her entire asset eventually left the family altogether in the form of charitable donations in her name to Yon-Sei University in Seoul.

Chapter Seven

Rites of Passage

In ninth grade, there was a bully named Kang-Pei at school, something that I had not yet encountered. He constantly harassed me for a month by hitting me a little too hard on the arm or shoulder, tripping me on steps, and even stealing my lunch. I tried talking to him, but that only made it worse. Discussing the problem with my teacher was not an option, as I would lose face among the entire class, people I would have to see every day for the next three years. After thinking of all the possible ways I could deal with him, I warned him to stop all contact or we would fight. Of course, he challenged me to a fight; and I could not back down. He agreed to meet me that Friday during lunch on top of the hill in the high school garden, far away from the sight of the teachers. I asked some friends to witness in case things got out of control; or in case he gang-attacked me with friends or used weapons. After an insufferable wait, Friday came; and about thirty boys gathered in a circle to watch me and Kang-Pei go at it. We started punching and kicking. He tagged me a few times on my face, but did not seriously injure me. I also inflicted minor damage on him. He sauntered around confidently like a boxer and had probably been a bully for years with much more experience in fighting. I was able to stay standing until the bell rang for class, at which time the fight had to end; unless we wanted to get in trouble with the headmaster. Eventually he disappeared altogether, probably expelled, but not before he taught me a valuable lesson in standing up to bullies, something I would do in other ways through military service later. Maybe the news of our scuffle reached the headmaster and prompted Kang-Pei's expulsion. Sometimes we do not have a choice but to fight violence with righteous use of force. I'll never forget how scared I was that day before the fight, fairly sure I'd get hurt by a bigger, stronger, and meaner adversary; but perhaps a more lasting impression was the self-contentment of having defended my honor and having staved off a menace.

Later that fall, my mother took me to a revival pilgrimage with several hundred spiritual seekers deep in the mountains of central Korea. We traveled in a caravan of open trucks through dense forests and rugged terrain on a challenging journey—a very Christianizing experience for most of them for the sheer physical challenges and discomfort of the voyage. I rode in the cab of the lead truck with Mother in relative comfort, very impressed with the earnest enthusiasm of the group, but did not have a conversion experience like the others. There was constant devotional singing, sometimes all through the night, along with spontaneous, fiery sermons and endless discussions about God, the Rapture, and the mysteries of the Holy Spirit. Some of the pilgrims, during the week of tent living, praying, and mountain hiking, were in bare feet and scanty clothing behaving like penitents, seeing images of Jesus, Mary, or John the Baptist. Several came down the mountain with raging eyes to proclaim their faith and themselves as eternal servants of God. At the time, I did not understand chastity, self-denial, and the rigors of monastic life, such as self-flagellation, all which seemed to be essential ingredients of their conversion experience.

One man clipped off all his hair and tore his clothes off in brash gestures, then smeared mud over his face while speaking in tongues in a disassociative-like state—yet with a strange smile on his face. Others walked backwards and recited scripture in unusual tones. Another woman, sweating profusely, grabbed me by the arms and looked deep into my eyes with her own crazed eyes and spoke in tongues. It sent chills deep through my spine. I felt as if I had been initiated into a secret order that few had the chance to see. I was amazed at their fervor and realized the power of spiritual faith. I was even more impressed by my mother's leadership and power to inspire the pilgrims, as they mourned and cried *"Halleluiah!"* and *"Amen!"* I think mother wanted me to see this soul-searching spectacle as part of my preparation for leaving Korea, as we had recently planned. These rites of passage were necessary to my evolution, as I would soon have no one to depend on but my own strength and personal faith for assurance in my upcoming transition.

Chapter Eight

Transpacific Passage

We all wanted me to go to America. It was a much-needed escape from my parents' discord, and promised Misa and me the best future. After all, look how well America had treated Uncle Ilhan! Father told me to keep an eye on my sister until she got to her orphanage in LA. and carefully sewed a $100 bill into the inner lining of my jacket, which I slept with and never let out of my site. I kept a close eye on Misa and braced myself for a long trip across the ocean. Dad stayed on the train with us until the last possible second and wept as he held me, the only time I had ever seen him cry. I had no idea at the time how little I would see of him the next seven years. In a way, I had not really grasped just how far away America was, and not just in physical distance.

On a cold December morning in 1956, I stood alone on the stern of an enormous cargo ship looking at the almost surreal mist-covered Golden Gate Bridge. It was the happiest moment of my life, a vision of my inevitable liberation as I dreamed of what awaited me in the great new world. Misa and I were the only passengers on the ship, and Father had told not to let her out of my sight, but she was too scared to come up on deck, so I slipped away for a few minutes to gaze on the vast panorama of sea and nearby coast. I was jolted from my reverie when the captain admonished me to get back inside, motioning to the heavy weather and fierce winds. But the majestic headlands of my promised California were in my system, and my heart had already leapt ashore and started its own life. I could actually feel my heart enlarge, and the beat accelerated as if it knew something I had yet to discover. Though I could not imagine what awaited me, I knew even at sixteen years old, I was being reborn, not unlike the first pilgrims that came to America, or the revival pilgrims I had seen deep in the mountains of Korea.

As planned, I met my adopted parents, Alma and Richard Gilmore, for the first time at the dock. This arrangement was made by my mother without soliciting my opinion. They drove all the way up from Glendale, a suburb of Los Angeles, to get me. Both were in their late '50s. He was pale, anemic, and chronically short of breath, having had a lung removed due to tuberculosis. His frailty and timidity were well compensated for by his vociferous and imposing wife who had a Wagnerian voice and weighing at least 250 pounds. Initially they were very cordial; and I would be cooperative throughout the next six months, speaking little and listening constantly, trying to discern my position in the family and new society, and trying to learn English as quickly as possible.

Saying goodbye to Misa, as we dropped her off at her orphanage on Sunset Boulevard was difficult, but the arrangements had been made for her to live here, and she would at least be safe. In spite of the fact that Mother and Uncle Ilhan arranged for him to adopt her so that she could come to America, nobody wanted Misa, so she was tossed into an orphanage for their unknown or selfish reasons. The adoption was solely for the purpose of getting her to America, which was ultimately good for her, though conducted irresponsibly my both my mother and uncle. At that moment, I recalled how Dad had urged me not to let Misa out of my sight, and now I had to hug her goodbye without knowing when I would see her next. She bravely held back her tears, and I had a lump in my throat as I drove off with the Gilmores.

After a brief drive through San Francisco, on a tour and stopping by a roadside café, we arrived at a rural home of her Swedish relatives near San Jose. They had a teenage daughter, Kathleen, about sixteen years old. All of them were naturally expressive, somewhat boisterous and friendly, listening to music, playing board games. Later, Kathleen's mother suggested I take her daughter for a walk through the nearby woods. I was impressed by the girl's natural spontaneity in extending her hands freely for help whenever we crossed small streams—something I had never seen a Korean girl or woman do. She talked about music and Elvis Presley, then a famous draftee on his way to Germany. I had heard of his electric performances and girls rioting when he played, but only heard his music for the first time that night when she played "Money Honey" for me and did a little twist-dance to show me how Elvis moved. As we talked, I felt increasingly comfortable, relieved, and accepted. This affirmed my hopes of America as a great and promising nation that were largely formed in my mind by movies like "Elmer Gantry," "I confess" American soldiers, my missionary neighbors, and the amazing machines and construction projects I'd seen during and after the war. As I sat in their living room and observed their lively conversations, I felt as if I was in a dream, soon to wake up in my bed at my Father's house in Seoul.

The next day, we drove down to Glendale to the Gilmores' charming house on a small, isolated hill on one-fourth of an acre with green ground cover, shrubs,

I. DAVID HONG MD, US NAVY CAPTAIN, RETIRED

and a fenced dog pen in back. I was shown my room with a great garden view downstairs. After unpacking, I thanked them for a wonderful drive and tour from San Francisco, and presented the gifts I had brought from my father's prized antique collection: two valuables ancient Korean hexagonal vases. I also gave Alma the $100 bill that my father had sewn into my jacket lining to hold for me in case of an emergency. The next few days passed quickly as I studied English and set to my chores which included changing the thickly spread soiled newspapers put down every night in Alma's bedroom, where her two growling Chow dogs slept. Mr. Gilmore slept in his own bedroom and seemed content to keep a considerable distance from her at all times. Unlike the Cocker Spaniels I raised as a child, all my attempts to befriend these canines with food and kindness failed. Later I learned that it is characteristic of Chows to befriend only one master and be standoffish to all others. Not even my soft-spoken, one-lunged adopted father could gain the good favor of these dogs. I also maintained the grass and grounds of the large hillside in the backyard, a job I enjoyed.

CHAPTER NINE

Escape!

Within two weeks, I excitedly enrolled at Glendale High School, selecting almost entirely English-related courses: spelling, grammar, typing, business English, and a Shakespeare class. I also took trigonometry in hope to make a point. I knew that to make any progress and to avoid being a burden, I must master English. One thing that my short life in war-torn Korea had showed me was that the definition of intelligence was the ability to adapt, and I often thought about the fate of the dinosaurs and imagined I might share it if I did not adjust quickly. Though I could not express much, I worked hard and badly wanted to get an A in trigonometry, which would be a way of introducing myself to the others, since I could not converse well. It was important to show that I possessed redeeming qualities, as I was still a burden to talk to, could not play football or other American games, and did not possess any obvious talent or good looks, at least by American standards. I was a poor, quintessential foreigner and had no illusions about my situation; but thought that if I could get at least a C in *anything*, they would know I was not an idiot. If I failed, I would then know my limits and plan accordingly. "This is not Korea," I would repeat to myself. If it were, my father would guide me, even provide for my livelihood.

It was around this time that I became unusually aware of the beating of my own heart. This became a spiritual companion to me, as I knew I was alone, but was also aware that God had spared me and provided for me many times. In profound, stark solitude, I knew I could get through the loneliest times, just as I had survived the abandonment of my mother and the chaos and poverty of war. I would lay my head on my pillow each night and listen to my heart drum away, like the Japanese Taiko drums my father so loved. I thought of him every night, often with tears. Even from a seemingly infinite distance, he was my ally in survival.

I got the A in trigonometry, however Shakespeare proved more difficult. In the final examination on *Hamlet*, I could not begin to answer the complicated question to "describe Hamlet's relationship to Polonius." I only understood a few pages of the play and decided to ignore the question and write from my memory of the "To be or not to be" soliloquy. Miss Burnside, the young English teacher later had the students comment on each other's work. When my essay came up, everyone was silent. She gave me a C; and I knew that I had not yet truly entered the culture, but was trying with everything I had.

The student body was entirely white with only a few dark-complexioned teachers, but they all showed interest in me and displayed kindness. Mark, a classmate, invited me to a party, but eventually lost interest when the language gap became too burdensome.

Then there was Gretchen who sat next to me by virtue of the alphabet in the Shakespeare course. She was tall and slender with long blonde hair and sometimes gave me a lot of attention. She had winked at me twice; and I had to ask a classmate what that meant, as it was a sign, we did not have in Korea. She gave me needed comfort in very many ways, and on her school picture wrote a genuinely kind note, signed "with love," which delighted me. I have kept that picture all these years, but at the time could not respond to her or tell her why I had to decline her many offers to go around town with her, as Mrs. Gilmore refused to let me ride the city buses alone. I was demoralized to have to refuse her invitations and lamented my lack of freedom to meet my peers outside of school. I began to question Mrs. Gilmore's motives for denying my freedom, and even her motives for adopting me. What had my mother done? Gretchen wrote me several times after I left the Gilmores; and I thought about her constantly, missing her kind face and reassurances. Several years later in 1964, after the first year from medical school in Nashville, I returned to Los Angeles at Christmas to see my sister's progress. I called Gretchen's home. Her mother answered and she recognized me instantly telling me that Gretchen was still in Michigan. To my surprise, she then extended invitation to her Christmas party at her home on coming Saturday. I accepted. On that evening, I drove higher and higher into winding picturesque Hollywood hills overlooking bright lights below ending to their well-decorated gate. Still I drove around upward through beautiful garden and a small cabin with a pond below and finally the entrance of the house. Gretchen's parents came out to greet me amongst more than a dozen guests. I have not yet experience in opulence, glitter, and grace. I learned he was the Hollywood scriptwriter.

I would dream of and remember Korea fondly, particularly the way that I enjoyed absolute freedom and the means to explore the countryside alone, riding the buses, trains, ox-carts, or my bike wherever I chose. I roamed all over the peninsula, visiting friends and distant relatives to bid farewell before my departure to America. With the Gilmores, I was not unlike a modern day abused child or spouse. An event that signaled my peak of despair over this stifling situation was when Mrs. Gilmore entered the bathroom while I was bathing in the tub and gave me a strange, prurient look for far too long and smiled—then excused her intrusion, saying she had to check the water or pipes, or something. I shouted at the top of my lungs for her to get out of the bathroom; and from that night on, there was a different atmosphere in the Gilmore house, as I truly did not feel part of it anymore. I knew I needed to make a move out of there soon. In retrospect, I think I should have consulted Gretchen about my problem. I tried to talk to my biology teacher but started crying; and he failed to follow through, nor did he refer me to a school counselor, if we even had one.

The Gilmores were isolated from society and did not even interact with their neighbors. Once in those six months, they had another childless couple over for dinner. I was painfully isolated and starved for interaction. They had no beliefs, religion, education, or sense of community—not even a simple hobby. One evening I brought up the subject of attending college and going to medical school. Alma said she did not believe it was possible for me to be a doctor in America; and that in fact, a college education was not necessary. I became acutely aware that the spiritual and emotional poverty of these people would continuously squelch my potential and began concocting plans for my escape.

Mr. Gilmore was passive-aggressive towards his wife, but mostly submissive to her. He was weak, but kind and sympathetic toward me. He had no control in the household and was utterly impotent and hesitant to engage me for fear of challenging her authority. With only one lung, he had no place to go; and his collusion with her was a matter of his survival. I will never forget his attempt to teach me Lincoln's Gettysburg Address, most of which I can still recite. We were both subjugated by the same tyrant.

I needed money and their permission to leave—neither of which would they have considered. I received less than a dollar per month in the form of a nickel a day for milk at school. I religiously stashed every single nickel in an old, rusty can in the tool shed for a few months, wondering what became of the $100 bill I entrusted to her upon my arrival. I did not ask for it, since she had told me some time ago that she had spent far more than that on me since my arrival. I started to blame myself for not insisting on meeting these people in person first before coming to live with them in America. I had wanted so badly to come, especially with the uncomfortable situation of my parents being divorced and their constant arguments as to who would pay my expenses and tuition, and being moved back and forth between their homes. I received no correspondence from the Gilmores before I left Korea, and had not even seen pictures of them.

I. DAVID HONG MD, US NAVY CAPTAIN, RETIRED

I did not tell anyone of my elaborate plan to run away, except my father in a somewhat panicked six-page letter written in red ink—the such letter I had written to him. I used red to convey the urgency and danger that I felt. I detailed my sadness and the decision to leave the Gilmores and confirmed my decision not to return to Korea until I had succeeded in America. More importantly, I conveyed my need for money for day-to-day living and upcoming college expenses. In the letter, I conducted a self-analysis and rehearsed my plan for action—a sort of catharsis for my father to witness my situation, as I felt incredibly isolated. I could not give the letter to Alma to send for fear of questions as to its content, or the invasion of my privacy—or the possibility she would not send it at all. I also felt guilty for betraying them. I left the sealed letter on my neighbor's porch table with a note asking him to mail it since I did not have the means or money for postage, hoping he would intervene for me. Though we had not introduced ourselves, we had exchanged friendly glances over the months while we worked the grounds of the hillsides of our respective backyards. Luckily, my neighbor obliged, as I received a response three months later from my father. In those days, international surface mail took three months to send a letter and receive a response. Airmail, which was more expensive, took one month. Father abided and was sad and sympathetic in a short reply, conveying his trust in me. As I read the note, I remembered how we preserved each other amid the bombs and bullets in Korea, hand in hand across the countryside looking for food, fighting to survive, joined at the hip. I cried thinking of how he had mentored and protected me, shielded my little body with his at times, and fed me and my sisters the last of the stew time after time while he went hungry that terrible year in Korea.

One day while quietly reorganizing my belongings, I discovered a .22 rifle in the basement. I stopped for a while, remembering Dostoyevsky's *Crime and Punishment* and the murder of the old woman, trying to remember Raskolnikov's reason for slaying her. I was having the most bizarre thoughts of how to get free from my oppressor and frightened myself in the process. I decided to run away. I knew that I could survive on the streets having been hardened by the war for a while if necessary.

The first Saturday after the semester ended, I quietly disappeared on a city bus. At last, permitted to ride the forbidden bus! For the first time, I headed toward Sunset Boulevard; which I had heard so much about, but had never seen, near as it was to our home. I thought that the worst outcome would be to encounter a policeman—or would that be the best? Would they consider me a delinquent? I was in completely unknown territory, feeling like a criminal, but also liberated for the first time in America. I spent all day and into the evening on the Sunset Strip amazed by the cast of characters passing by. I was also looking for a safe and reasonable place to spend the night, which was fast approaching. I had little money and was anxious to meet someone who could rescue me. Earlier, while asking directions on the bus, I met a kind Swedish woman in her late '30s. She asked about my origins and the details of my situation and empathized with my being away from my homeland, like her. She invited me to her home for lunch and offered a temporary living arrangement, but her husband made her rescind when they spoke on the phone. She then dropped me off at the bus station with tears in her eyes. Meeting her confirmed again my hope in the basic goodness of Americans, their humanitarian sensibilities and genuine kindness.

I grew increasingly both worried and fascinated by this newfound freedom, walking and drinking in the sights all day with great interest in spite of my critical situation. As night approached, a different assortment of characters appeared: rougher looking types, other homeless men, prostitutes, con artists, drunks, lunatics, and hobos milling about. This was the true night scene of an American inner city, not unlike Seoul. Naturally, I felt sympathetic toward the other homeless. They seemed to accept me into that night's street community. A toothless man in frayed white cowboy hat gave me a hunk of stale bread. I did not feel threatened or in any way endangered, as I was strong from constant yard work and playing soccer at school. I also had been through a miserable war before and knew how to keep energy in reserve for a possible emergency battle or flight. My eyes had not been so wide open since I had gotten off of the boat.

By early dawn, I was hungry and desperate for shelter when a police car stopped in front of me. The cop got out and asked, "Are you hungry?" I answered yes, and he invited me to a hamburger shop on Vine and Sunset two blocks away. I had a few dollars, but did not want to spend any. The officer saw my hesitation when I looked at the menu and assured me the meal was on the police department. I filled up on two delicious cheeseburgers; and he suggested we go to the station, to which I agreed with relief. Obviously, the Gilmores had called in, as the police already knew about me; but the officer asked for more details, and I told him about my problems with the Gilmores, my enrollment at Glendale High, and my desire to go to an orphanage. They kept me in a large room where I could sleep a little and write on a desk. After a few hours, three more officers came in, and then had a closed conference. I wrote a one-line note: *"Where there is a will there is a way"* and gave it to one of the officers. When police chief returned with a big smile, but without a social worker, only uniformed officers, I told them I was unwilling to go back to the Gilmores. Still, an hour later, they asked me if I wanted to back to Korea, to which I gave on a scrap paper, "If were dead, dead!" That must have scared them; and they turned to each other and shrugged, seeming to understand my concept of honor.

I told them how I enjoyed visiting the orphanage in Korea and was impressed by the programs they had, including visits from American soldiers who brought gifts for the kids. Once they brought a pair of Yorkshire pigs, bigger than they brought any I had seen before. After, the chief told me there was no choice but to go back to the Gilmores until they could arrange an orphanage. I refused again, and the officer asked, "Would you like to come stay with my family?" Somehow I misunderstood and did not accept his offer—something I regretted for a long time after. I was too tired and embarrassed to ask the details of what he was offering. I wish there would have been a social worker there to shed some light on my options and to interpret what the officer meant. I was so confused and distressed, and cannot even remember if I thanked him. The chief mentioned Boy's Town in Nebraska, about which I knew nothing. I told him I liked Glendale High and would like to stay nearby. I agreed to go back to the Gilmores' with the agreement that it was temporary until a suitable orphanage was found. In the late afternoon, the Gilmores came to pick me up and took me back to their home. There were no demands, punishment, or pressure from them—only complacency—something I had grown used to. Only later did I learn that Mr. Gilmore had a longstanding relationship with the juvenile division of the Glendale police and that he was a desk clerk.

One morning about three weeks later, the Gilmores told me, we were going somewhere without saying where, and I did not ask. I packed and they dropped me off at the Spanish American Institute (SAI), a Methodist orphanage, vocational school on Figueroa Street in Gardena, about twenty miles from Glendale, where I would live for the next three years.

CHAPTER TEN

A New Life at the Spanish American Institute (SAI), an Orphanage

SAI occupied four city blocks and housed around 120 displaced boys from junior high to college level from Mexico, Cuba, and Central and South America. Most of them spoke only Spanish, except a few black kids. The staff was from diverse backgrounds and spoke several languages. There were suddenly a whole new cast of characters in my life; and some of them would alter my path significantly for the better, providing me with an opportunity to have all that I could hope for.

Sister Frieda wore a black habit and spoke with a hopelessly thick German accent. She often invited me to practice German with her. She looked down on the other disorganized, unclean boys and their crude manners, and obsessively cleaned the floors and bathrooms with boundless energy. She would tell me that I was different than the other boys, that I had a look of "nobility." I had to look up the word, and could not help but think of my ancestors from the old country and the tales I heard of the glorious court of Genghis Khan, or the old Chosun kingdom and all its majesty.

Dr. Ester, an aging Methodist theologian, had retired on the campus to meditate and lived in a charming detached cottage. She often invited me often for afternoon English tea and shared her metaphysics. I read books in her books in the midafternoon in her comfortable refuge—the only air-conditioned building in all of SAI, which could get unbearably hot in the summer. I devoured books from her library; and as I read, would ask her questions about the English language and the content of the books. She was refined, from a prominent religious family whose proud tradition made me curious. I read Emerson's essays and other

I. DAVID HONG MD, US NAVY CAPTAIN, RETIRED

Transcendentalists with great curiosity, and she would explain the finer points. Her place was decorated with family heirlooms, antique china, silver platters, and prized landscape paintings. She often led the pre-meal prayers in fluent Spanish for all the boys in the dining hall. I was always protective of her, as the other orphans abused her with tricks, snickers, jeers, and endless crude jokes.

There was a Filipino grounds worker named Jose, a low-ranking retiree from the US Navy who would tell me about his adventures in the Pacific Theater—great tales of war against the fearsome Japanese fighter planes. He worked the flower gardens with silent precision and pride that caught my attention. I studied him closely as I calculated my chances for realizing my dreams of medical school as a foreigner. It was good to see immigrants from other nations and how they worked to get up the ladder, particularly those that did so by serving the righteous cause of World War II.

There was another religious couple from the Midwest, the Bronsons, who lived as resident houseparent in the dorm. She was an enormous blonde, over 200 pounds, and very sociable and helpful. They appeared to be in near poverty, but were very proud; as he was a fourteenth generation descendant of George Washington and loved singing the "Battle Hymn of the Republic" which he taught me. Next ten years, I sang, quietly to myself and loudly in church services, the same verses many a times until I became an MD. Upon reflection, I can now see that I could not have been exposed to a better cross section of the real America than I was at SAI.

Dr. and Mrs. Silverthorne, the SAI directors, had been missionaries in Malaysia and were reassigned to America a few years before I came to SAI. Dr. Silverthorne was frail and skinny and wore thick glasses and was always running around—impressively energetic for a man in his mid '60s. He was and immediately very fond of me, and I knew I had a true guardian in him. It was an instant sense of trust, even though there would be some episodes for us to overcome in the following years. Mrs. Silverthorne was plump, blonde Christian woman in her late '50s. She played beautiful hymns on the piano every Sunday in the chapel and became my self-appointed guardian, quietly keeping SAI going behind the scenes. She gave me countless hours of help when I was working on special projects for at SAI. There were three boys, including me, as emissaries to communities to participate in their churches in suburbs on Sunday services to sing and talk about SAI.

Gardena was prototypical working class America. The high school student body was about 15% second generation Japanese, and the rest was white. SAI had its own bus to the schools, so I missed the opportunity to interact with the "regular" students from the community. On the SAI bus, they only spoke loud Spanish among themselves, leaving me feeling disconnected. Even after later learning

Spanish in Junior College, finding common ground with the Spanish-speaking boys was difficult. The students from Gardena High were somewhat put off by the Spanish-only attitude of the SAI boys, so they were somewhat discriminated against. Most people just assumed I was Japanese.

As soon as I finished one semester at Gardena High, surprisingly to me in the senior class, I received a notice to make an appointment with a career counselor who told me I could graduate after next semester. The pace hastened faster than I expected. One of the students in the school had a father who was a respected doctor in town, and I called and was allowed to visit Dr. Kobeyashi's office and observe his medical practice. I had heard that medical doctors had the most independence, social prestige, and highest standard of living in America then; and I remembered throughout human history, from the Egyptians to now, medicine men and priests were the most important people in society except for the kings.

When I arrived to Dr. Kobeyashi's reception area, there were about fifteen patients waiting. A third was Japanese and the rest were Caucasian. He had a large staff and a dozen rooms all humming with activity. In all, some two dozen people revolved around him; and he seemed to have complete control of his office and his life, along with knowledge, wealth, and social status. What could be better than gaining complete control of my life in a similar fashion? Things had been in disarray since my arrival and this lifestyle looked like an extremely attractive option instead of my original plan to be an architect rebuilding war-torn Seoul. After the appointment, I had to walk four miles back to SAI, a good opportunity to see the city and neighborhoods. I found a secondhand store selling decent clothes and a used bicycle—which I badly needed.

I knew the only way to make my future was to graduate from college, which was expensive. Therefore, I thought the only way to college was to get As to receive a scholarship. Grades became my next five-year obsession. It was funny that I was so concerned about tuition, because public colleges were relatively cheap, and I learned later that many students like me graduated from college while working part-time. Even better was the GI Bill, which paid tuition and minimum living expenses for all who served in uniform. I could not conceive of such affordable education; because in Korea, all forms of school required tuition. I worked hard, competing with a dozen declared premed majors at Gardena High in the most difficult science courses. Dr. Goldberg's physics class was known to be a killer; but to everyone's surprise, I got an A. Early the next semester, the school counselor called me in to tell me I could graduate in January, saying I would do fine in college. But where? It was too late to apply for a scholarship, so I decided to wait and graduate in June and go on to nearby Compton Junior College, which did not require tuition. The pace frightened me; but it occurred to me that I had skipped three grades thus far: the second grade for an unknown reason, the fifth grade due to the war, then eleventh grade in the process of coming to America.

For months, I had the demoralizing problem of having no spending money. I needed a dollar a week for paper and pencils. I did not return pencils and pens I found at school, and rummaged through the wastebasket for paper with one side still blank—good enough for turning in homework. At least the orphanage had an inexhaustible supply of staple food. US government butter came in huge boxes; bread arrived almost daily by the truckload, and meat arrived endlessly in huge refrigerated trucks. To my shock, half the food that was left over at SAI was thrown away! This I knew because like all the boys, I had to work shifts in the kitchen and dining hall and regular schedule milking at dawn. Fresh vegetables and fruits were rare, most likely due to the extra labor involved. I always wondered why the vegetables were so overcooked to the point of disintegration. One day while washing dishes in the kitchen, I asked the overweight, bossy black cook, and she chastised me saying, "You just keep eating!

Chapter Eleven

The Smell of Hard-earned Money

When my financial desperation became unbearable, one fine Saturday morning after a heavy SAI breakfast, I left the orphanage and walked a few blocks into the residential area to look for a job. When I saw a couple working in their yard, I offered my labor, got the job easily and worked hard for three hours, earning two dollars for the first time in my life. I accepted their invitation to lunch, after which the man went into his attic and found two old, dusty English grammar books, among others to give me. Those first two dollars smelled so good! I kept my hand in my pocket, fondling the crisp bills all the way home with an exhilarated bounce in my step. They invited me back to work again, confirming my hope that America offered unlimited promise. I always had inexhaustible energy from the great quantities of surplus food I consumed, wolfing down enormous meals to maintain energy reserves for longer duration. I also ate fast to save time, and according to my wife have maintained these habits. My family tells me that I still have the same habit.

The next Saturday, I tried another place to see how much they would pay me and found yard work again on my first try. While I was busy and sweaty in the garden, an attractive girl about my age in a bright green sun dress came out of the house and offered me a Coke, which I had tried only once before. She had a brilliant, generous smile, so angelic that I thought maybe I was dreaming. I drank the Coke and watched her ease back to the house, trying to negotiate the strange feeling that had come over me. My skin was tingling and my heart swelled. Maureen came back later with another Coke and a tuna sandwich and looking directly into my eyes, asked me on a date. I told her I did not have a car and pointed to the orphanage three blocks away, sure that would end her interest. She was not deterred and turned the charm on even more, brushing her skin against mine from time to time, as we spoke. She was nearly as tall as me with long, dark hair and a cute little turned-up nose and full lips that I would soon not stop thinking about. We agreed to meet the next night at seven; and I slept poorly for the first time in months, wondering what I would say on our date and how I would be able to impress an American girl.

When I arrived on foot the next evening, Maureen came quickly outside while her parents, to my surprise, stood by the door and waved, apparently giving their blessing. I did not know where to go on foot, except back to the SAI barn where all of us orphans had to work two hours every day. It turned out to be a fun place to go for a first date, and we quickly were at ease with each other. She was amused when I told that a Holstein in the far stall had side-kicked me when I went to milk her the other morning at 5 a.m. I showed her the painful bruise on my left thigh. She laughed even harder when I demonstrated how I was less than kind to the poor cow to whom I was venting my frustration. We explored the haystack, scattering hay on the chickens and goats. The moon was bright and the stars sparkled more crisply then I had ever seen. It was the first time I had been so close to a girl, and was beside myself with desire. I kissed her by the tool rack and could feel her heart beating when I held her. Soon we were pressed against rakes and pitchforks that were hanging from the wall, but barely noticed the discomfort as we dove into each with abandon and fell to the hay-strewn ground. She finally confessed to me later that she was in my graduating class at Gardena High and had seen me often at school, and I felt embarrassed for not having recognized her.

Now that I had got a taste of work outside the orphanage, I wanted more and responded to an LA newspaper ad for a sales job downtown. I arrived by bus the next Saturday near Watts, where a distinguished middle-aged black man interviewed and hired me on commission to sell Fuller brushes door-to-door in a racially mixed, but mostly black area. It was a new experience to spend all day with black families. I walked miles with my large bag of brushes, but sold little. I tried one more Saturday, and I knew I was no good at sales. I became intrigued with meeting people of different ethnicities around LA and hitchhiked between town and Gardena, checking out different neighborhoods. It was easy to get rides. It was good experience to see how some minorities lived.

My next easy job was cleaning a Chinese restaurant every Friday and Saturday at 10 p.m. after closing. It was a chance to eat good Chinese food, which I missed. Just the thought of working there made my mouth water and cinched my decision: the smell of garlic shrimp, steamed bok choy, noodles, and Asian spices reawakened my soul. I commuted on my five-dollar secondhand a bicycle that I had fixed it up with some tools I borrowed from the Mexican boys who worked on their cars a lot. I rode that bike for two years.

Every Friday and Saturday night just before 10 p.m. curfew, I slipped away into the darkness like a ghost; and no one knew that I worked except Sister Frieda who covered for me by ignoring my absence, since she understood my needs. We had bonded listening to Grofe's *Grand Canyon* in her room. I would quickly pedaled from SAI into the darkness, arriving at the restaurant, ate to my heart's content, and quickly clean the place to get back to SAI shortly before midnight. Of course, I was not the only one sneaking out on Saturday nights, but probably the only one doing so to work!

This plan worked well for four months until one midnight on the way back to the orphanage when a Gardena police car with flashing lights stopped me for a headlight violation. The officer wanted to know where I was coming from and why I was riding so fast in complete darkness, suspecting, I think, some sort of robbery. When he demanded information, I told him I was a senior at Gardena High and pointed to the orphanage where I lived explaining that I needed to work weekend nights to buy school supplies. I gave the names of my teachers and he seemed to relax. I told him not to worry about me. He understood and visibly changed his attitude, insisting on accompanying me to the orphanage, which I told him was unnecessary, since there was hardly any traffic that time of night. He followed me all the way to the front door of the dormitory anyway. The next day, Mr. Silverthorne called me into the office telling me that he received a call from the police, and that it was illegal for a minor to work at night, and that I could not leave the orphanage at night for work, or anymore I could not tell him that I needed money for school supplies.

I continued my routine and did my homework diligently, working out some of my frustrations fooling around in the barn. I still had extra energy on the weekends, but no place to go. I then found a cowboy supervisor to teach me how to ride and handle the horse. I befriended a stallion and in a week got on him, reluctantly and trembling, but determined not to show fear. I continued to improve my riding skills, and all seemed to go well until one day the horse got excited and brushed too close to the fence. I sustained a painful open wound to my leg, which I cleaned with soap and water. Mr. Howe from the SAI office thought I should go to the LA County Hospital. Then I took the downtown bus to the LA County Hospital and limped into the emergency room with great pain. I finally registered, took a number, and waited in a long line of nearly a hundred crying babies, elderly and mostly black people. This was only the second time I was seeing a doctor, but now for a different reason. I also saw for the first time what it was like in the black ghetto. After two hours, I saw a young, sympathetic doctor who cleaned the wound, stitched it, and assured me I would be fine. I followed his instructions and healed within a few days.

Chapter Twelve

Devastating Disappointment

It had been several months since I wrote the red-ink letter of despair to my father asking for money to liberate me from the Gilmores and help get me enrolled in college. I knew he would understand. I was overjoyed when I received his reply saying that he was selling his last spare lot next to the house in order to help support me.

One day I received a call from a stranger who identified herself as a missionary returning from Korea saying that she had $700 for me from my father. I knew he would do his best to smuggle money into the US for me. In the old days, and even now, many poor countries forbade taking dollars out, as they were badly needed to import essentials. My father's gift would assure my living expenses and tuition for the next semester. The missionary lady was very polite and proper, clearly saying that she left the money at the SAI office since I was still a minor. She gave the money to my legal guardian, Dr. Silverthorne. I suddenly felt sick and literally could not stomach this news. I immediately dashed to the office to see Dr. Silverthorne who explained to me that neither the Gilmores nor anyone else had paid for my room and board for over a year—$100 a month, but no one was obligated to pay if I was in financial hardship. Now that there was money available, the orphanage was entitled to it! I was speechless and profusely tearful, and even perplexed by an unjust system that seemed intent on denying me my freedom. It seemed as though I simply was not allowed to have any assets whatsoever, from the $100, that Mrs. Gilmore took, to the inability to work at night, and now this—not even money from my own father for college. I left the room having received an education in the power of the law.

This was the first time that I was amazed by the American legal system, something I would revisit in many different contexts over the next forty years.

This time it was to my disadvantage, but it would not always be. I accepted $700 loss with more tears alone many nights, but I decided not to tell my father of the episode for fear of burdening him in his declining health. I never asked anything from him again. Still, I was in a bind and could not beg for money from Mr. Silverthorne, nor did he even offer a few dollars—and he looked very uncomfortable about the situation, almost letting on that he saw the injustice in this too. I should have asked for some small amount at least; but as a minor and a foreigner with no adults to trust to look after my interests, I was completely powerless. I learned the American meaning of "the letter of the law." Thirty years later, I learned that the property that he sold for $700 was valued at $700,000!

The Gilmores came and took me out for a hamburger twice over the next two years, but never offered even modest assistance. I should probably have asked them for spending money, but my pride kept me from doing so. Each time I saw them, I remembered the $100 father had lovingly sewed in my coat lining that survived my voyage all the way to America, only to be misappropriated by my own guardians who never offered me a cent or even contributed to my orphanage fees. I could not bring myself to address the issue and knew it would be fruitless anyway. From then on, I decided to trust myself only. The Gilmores, nonetheless, seemed to be pleased by my good progress, but failed to respond in any manner when I announced my plans to go to college. Neither of them went to college nor valued education. When I invited them to my high school graduation ceremony, they did not respond. Mr. Gilmore died shortly after that; and she moved into a small house in the Watsonville hills, miles from the nearest neighbor. Five years later, I would drive up to visit.

Alma was pleased to see me and seemed unchanged, but with two new Chows, and still drinking vodka every night. I noticed the prominently displayed antique Korean vases on her mantle that I would presented them seven years before. Ten more years later, while in the service overseas in service, I received notice of her passage. I had long ago forgiven her negligence.

Sundays were always busy at SAI. Dr. Silverthorne usually asked me and another boy or two to participate in 11:00 services or other church programs in outlying communities, including the Quakers in Pasadena. At this church, I met an immigration lawyer who later would help facilitate my naturalization based on conscientious objector.

At my first Christmas service at SAI in 1957, Betsy Silverthorne, always urgent in her manner, was eager to decorate the buildings and organize our performance of the nativity scene with the three wise men in full costume. She directed the play while hiding behind a painted screen, looking through a small hole to guide the boys on stage. Like in church, there was much singing from hymnals and other sources, accompanied by Mrs. Silverthorne's piano. While Mr. Silverthorne was the director of SAI, she had the true unspoken talent for leadership and led behind the scenes. The advent play was a sort of family affair in which all the boys were expected to be either in the audience or on stage, according to their inclination or talent. This is where I learned to sing, work through my sorrows, and restore my perspective through plays and the music of the masters. I continued taking voice classes for many years and later joined a memorable opera production of Stravinsky's *Rake's Progress*, directed by Dr. DeClauqq from Switzerland at USC, whom I got to know while being part of the crew and observing the operations of a full-scale opera production.

    The Silverthornes continued to show great affection and generosity to me and expressed extreme happiness with my grades and overall performance. He told me that I had been selected as one of the three oratory contestants for the upcoming biannual fundraiser—the biggest event of the institution. A few hundred prominent guests from greater Los Angeles were to come to the orphanage, and prominent judges would choose the winner of the contest. Betsy volunteered to coach me on my content and delivery to help my chances. Meanwhile they asked me to work in their house for a few hours every Saturday for the same pay that he gave the other employees, as opposed to me having to go outside of SAI to find work. I happily accepted and started feeling more of a sense of belonging at the orphanage. The more help that I received from the Silverthornes, and as I witnessed their incredible selfless dedication to SAI and orphans like me, the less resentful I felt about losing my $700—and now can see that the opportunities they afforded me. These institutions are still in dire need of public and private funding and essential to a cohesive society.

    I worked every Saturday for the next three months; and they were happy to have me in their home, trusting me completely, unlike others. I kept their house clean and orderly while they were away. While I housesit, I would read from their library and answer calls, becoming familiar with their whole family. There was no guardedness whatsoever between us—just unspoken mutual trust and respect; and I became a de facto member of the family, learning all of their internal affairs and intimate particulars. When my cleaning work was finished, Betsy and I often spent many hours rewriting and practicing the text for my oration for the fundraiser, titled "Abraham Lincoln for All." The Silverthornes retired two years later, but our relationship continued many years through letters and extended visits I made to their creek-side cabin in Aptos, near Carmel Valley. We wrote to each other regularly until they passed away and still think of them often with pleasant memories . . .

Chapter Thirteen

The Doors Begin to Open

One Saturday in the spring of 1958, some 400 guests from all over southern California came to SAI to meet the residents, tour the grounds, and see the vocational programs in action, such as printing, weaving, carving, and leather working. The city guests enjoyed the extensive farm operations, including the dairy cows, which we milked for our own consumption. The highlight of the day was the oratory contest in the afternoon.

After preparing for three months, I won first place. SAI raised $75,000 that day and I became something of a local celebrity, as my talk, aimed at addressing core American values, went over very well and my life catapulted into a higher orbit from that day on for some years. I received frequent invitations to social events and visits to various patrons of SAI at their homes over weekend.

Once, an unusually attractive red-haired woman, who we later discovered was a Hollywood actress, visited and took me to lunch. I remember having a fantasy of achieving the ultimate social status of the Hollywood elite, being whisked away by the starlet and flaunted in public as one of LA's best and brightest—perhaps getting a bit part in a movie as well! I received another invitation to attend the *Nutcracker* by the Bolshoi Ballet from Moscow at the Paramount Theatre downtown. In those days, I kept a long list of all my contacts and teachers, in hopes that I might use them as references for medical school. Through all these invitations, dinners, and shows with influential people, I took the opportunity to witness how successful people thought and lived, studying their habits and beliefs with great care. I learned that "you are what you eat" in terms of social discourse and interaction as well as one's literal diet. I decided that if I associated with doctors, I had a better chance of becoming one. I knew whom I wanted to associate with and whom I wanted to leave behind—easier said than done when you are a minority and an orphan. This is why it was so critical for me to flee from the Gilmores, and the time was coming soon to leave SAI as well.

Sometime after Christmas that year, I was baptized at SAI Chapel by Dr. Silverthorne and Reverend John Black, president of Southern California Methodist Conference, who had been at the fundraising and oratory contest as I had requested two months earlier at SAI Chapel. This was a significant day for me, as I was becoming more and more interested in exploring the field of ministry.

The following spring, I received a mysterious invitation through the SAI front office to join twenty-three other college-bound students on a journey into the Sierra Nevada wilderness for two weeks following high school graduation. This would be one of the most memorable experiences of my life and my first true excursion across the American countryside. In June of 1958, I departed with two other students from outside communities with a parent for Bishop, CA, through the San Joaquin Valley. Near Bakersfield, we encountered hundreds of mightily pumping crude oil derricks, reminding me of the American industrial power that first astounded me in Korea. The sheer scale, size, and number of them sprouting like a gargantuan forest out of the desert sand impressed me. At Bakersfield there was an increase of temperature to over one hundred degrees and the flora changed dramatically—the first time I had seen desert landscape. It was good to be enjoying this in the company of well-bred friends my age, and with whom I had so much in common. There were unending flat verdant farms on either side of the highway laid out in perfect geometry to the horizon. The vastness of the irrigated land made me imagine the scale of government surplus food that we had been voraciously eating at SAI. We passed Modesto and Fresno and arrived at the base camp at the foothills of the Sierra Nevada near Bishop where our group met in a large cabin for a detailed orientation.

After a restful night, we responded to the call of the pristine Sierras. All of the student participants, guides, staff members, a nurse, a packhorse driver, and two ministers set out for the wilderness with great excitement. I recognized of the ministers was Dr. John Black, the bishop who baptized me several months ago at SAI. As soon as he greeted me with his infectious, bright smile, I knew where the invitation had come from. I was excited to get acquainted with my camp-mates too, a total of twelve young men and women, all from southern California.

We eventually reached the summit at 14,000 feet after ten days of hiking through rugged, beautiful passages above tree line and ever-changing flora and fauna. I was particularly fascinated by our sturdy packhorses that hauled our supplies for fourteen days—a sight I had only seen in western movies. I wanted to ride the horses since I was recently practiced at the SAI ranch. My camp-mates were all vigorous, articulate, and good-looking. I was so excited that, even after a hard day of hiking it was hard to sleep.

These two weeks were like a chapter from Chaucer's Canterbury Tales. Each of us assumed a role befitting our inclination. The first day was particularly hard, as climbing took its toll on some of the kids by late afternoon; and the hardening of our bodies was only beginning. Some girls had trouble carrying their packs and trailed far behind. We had a peaceful lunch near a glacial stream, and I was amazed at the lucid colors and crisp sounds of the alpine environment. By midafternoon, some kids had developed bad blisters and were unable to carry their packs. I volunteered by doubling the weight in my pack, as I could endure more than the others because I had gotten tough from the farm work. I could not help forming a satisfied smirk, as I thought, "Thank god for the hard labor I have done to prepare for this expedition." The first evenings we unloaded our supplies and set up a common area, sharing communal dinners. Dr. Black suggested we each find a partner to share a tent with for the duration of the trip. Ed, the jovial son of a Christian couple from El Segundo, with piercing blue eyes proposed we share; and I agreed. We would talk into the early hours about our hopes and troubles amid the night sounds of the alpine wilderness and brilliant shimmering stars.

There was a German girl, Sigrid, the daughter of a perished U-boat captain who had come alone to the US. We were kindred spirits, sharing the same fascination with the wilderness, excited about our immediate future. We climbed deeper into forest and higher mountain range. The second day went a little better as it got cooler in the ascent. There was a lot of talk about the previous night's disturbance in which Sigrid and several of the girls complained to the ministers that some boys moved too close to their tents. The ministers suggested we elect two cochairmen from the group to arbitrate the concerns of the concerned. I was surprised to be nominated by my peers as one of the cochairmen, although I still had significant difficulty speaking effective English. After a few hours of discussions, we resolved the conflict and the expedition resumed in even better spirits then it had started.

The next afternoon, I followed Reverend Wirth, the other minister, to trout fish in the stream with makeshift fly rods we constructed from tree branches. We caught several and brought them back to camp to clean and cook. It was among the most satisfying meals of my entire life, and I became a trout-fishing aficionado. To this day, I get goose bumps when I fly fish in Washington State. Resting on a pile of dry pine needles, looking into the shimmering firmament with complete awe, I fell asleep that night by the fire in a state of perfect contentment, and then was only awakened by the cheerful stirring of friends in the crisp, sunny morning. The majesty of the towering mountains was more inspiring each day. The sound of the rushing streams and squawks of magpies seemed to portend continuous magical messages of a higher order. The final sweat-drenched hiking day was capped off by a brave plunge into the 13,000 foot high glacial lake—a profound baptismal, and how appropriate to take this baptism next to the man that had baptized me in church a few months earlier. I felt as if I was now a true child of this amazing land that had adopted me.

That summer I decided to petition for citizenship and noticed on the form there was also a registration for the draft. Scarred as I was from the horrors of the war in my home country, I knew I could not participate in violence or killing, no matter what the circumstances and checked the box for "conscientious objector." I soon found that I would need a lawyer to make my case in court if I wanted to become a citizen. The Quaker lawyer that I had met through SAI as a volunteer at his church a few months earlier took my case, but it would cost me $300, so I would have to work extra hours to pull this off. I was given a date at the Federal District Court and stated my case before the judge. I can still see his long, serious face to this day. It would take over two years for me to obtain my American citizenship.

Chapter Fourteen

College Days

It was a good decision to attend Compton College, not that I had any other real options. It was only six miles from SAI, whereas UCLA was thirty-five miles away, and USC was fourteen miles. I learned to hitchhike and easily got to school that way, rather than bicycling, which was far too dangerous on the highway. With at least two books in my arms advertising that I was a student, I would cross Figueroa St., and stand westbound to get one mile to Artesia Blvd., an industrial area. From there it took only a couple of minutes to get another ride to the college. I did the same thing on the way back in the evening and repeated this routine for two years. Back then, it seemed that almost everyone stopped to offer a ride, often dropping me right at the front gate of SAI.

At Compton, I took premed science courses starting with inorganic, then organic chemistry, German and more English. Once I learned English, German came easier for me that it did for most of the Americans—a way for me to get the badly needed As on my transcript. I took Spanish the next semester, trying to keep those As coming so as to get a scholarship to a bigger college for my third an fourth year, and to be able to communicate with my fellow orphans at SAI. After the first semester, with an A average, I got a $300 Rotary scholarship which paid for all my school supplies.

I was busier in college than in high school and had less time for outside work, though I still needed more money. I applied for and got a part-time job working the grounds on the Compton campus. I was the youngest employee of the crew, and the only part-timer. It was a bit embarrassing sometimes to be seen by all my classmates working the campus grounds. Then I would thumb back to SAI after school, getting rides from quiet, almost apologetic commuters. I still felt anonymous in my new country, as if I did not even exist. I felt like I often fled my body after those long days of classes and grounds work, with only the beat of my heart to keep my spirit and body together as I stuck my thumb out at dusk. At the same time, though I was lonely at this point, I knew that my dreams were going to be fulfilled.

While I worked hard, I made it a point to have fun and took a classical music appreciation course and a singing class. The singing class required a campus recital for the final grade—at which I sang Nat King Cole's "Tenderly."

> *"The evening breeze caressed the trees tenderly.*
> *The trembling trees embraced the breeze tenderly.*
> *Then you and I came wandering by and lost in a sigh were we.*
> *The shore was kissed by the sea and mist tenderly.*
> *I cannot forget how two hearts met breathlessly.*
> *Your arms open wide and closed me inside.*
> *You took my lips; you took my love so tenderly . . ."*

It brought vigorous applause and my vocal teacher was proud. As I sang from the stage, I noticed a bejeweled beauty with incredible green eyes and auburn hair clapping in the back. She was a classmate from Spanish class named Charlotte, and I would not get her out of my mind for the next several months.

Charlotte sat alphabetically beside me in Spanish class—a beautiful bespectacled girl with stylish clothes and an intoxicating vanilla fragrance about her. Amid awkward conjugations, I stirred hopelessly with desire and curiosity. I seldom bought textbooks because I had only few dollars in my pocket, and they were freely available in the library. I remained intentionally bookless in Spanish, anticipating when we would next be asked by the professor to look into our books where I then got to nudge close to her, as she always gave me permission, coyly obliging over the course of the semester. There was always the slight suggestion of a smile on her lips, and she looked immaculate and dignified. To me she was a princess beyond compare and shone brighter than all of the pretty girls on campus. Sometimes, holding the book between us with trembling hands, our eyes would meet and our pupils dilated as we exchanged a few measured words. I did not know how strong her feelings were for me until she wrote me a beautiful letter of confession from Tulsa, Oklahoma, while I was working at the California Migrant Ministry the summer following graduation. She was the Beauty and I was the Beast.

There was another friend at Compton College; a friendly and fun-loving young man named Barry who was few years older than, already slightly balding and attending college on the GI Bill. One day he arrived in a brand new Triumph convertible, cruising around the parking lot to show off. He then invited me to drive down to Bakersfield and Palm Springs the following Saturday. Barry seemed to epitomize the American freedom through American movies and magazines that we all saw in the early '50s. He kept that car meticulously clean, as he kept himself.

Cruising in Barry's convertible became a ritual; and the following spring break, he and I and another friend with a Porsche headed to Palm Springs again, often racing at high speed. Then we went on to Nogales, Texas, into Mexico to go snorkeling a few days in the crystal waters of the reefs off Guaymas on the shores off of the Gulf of California. I saw my first stingrays and man-sized sharks there, which scared the daylights out of me. It was fun racing over the potholes through scattering goats and chickens on the rural Mexican roads, another first in my life—to drive a top-notch sports car.

I graduated from Compton with honors, but did not attend the ceremony, as I had to work. Just before graduating, I received notice of a full tuition scholarship to USC, just as I had hoped. It seemed like everything was rolling my way.

Chapter Fifteen

My First Job in Science

After two consecutive chemistry classes, I went on a job-hunt in a technical field, needing to get away from manual labor for a while. I had noticed a small, busy shop named the Polychemical Technical Institute (PTI) several blocks from SAI. One Saturday morning, I noticed only one car parked in the lot and the office door slightly open. Armed with my two semesters of stellar grades and a window of confidence that day, I knocked on the door and met the owner, Alex Silver, who was reading the *Tao De Ching* with a can of beer on his desk. I found it interesting that a chemist that produced industrial polymer glues would have a first century BC religious text in his hands.

He produced plastic and acrylic glues for the US Air Force for aircraft repair. After examining my transcript and asking me a few questions, he offered me a position as a research assistant—my first "real" job in science. In the fall of 1959, I started earning about $2.50 an hour with regular increases and ended up working there for four years until I graduated from USC.

Alex was an American Jew with a philosophy degree from USC, and one of the most beautiful person I've ever met, as he was always searching for the highest truth and spoke with great respect, as if he were speaking directly to their souls and always hungry for their ideas of truth. After I worked there a months, he invited me to his home in San Pedro for dinner. He lived in simple abundance, somewhat stoic, always struggling with philosophical and ethical questions. In time I had the master key of the compound; and I would often find him in his office after midnight, book in hand, beer on desk, gesticulating to an imagined partner in discourse with faint movements on his lips.

While he was in the service, he had married a Scottish woman; and they had four children. I had never met a Jewish person before; but it seemed that the further

I went into education, particularly medicine, I became surrounded by them. Alex, like was not at all orthodox and in fact philosophical and spiritual person. I never saw a Star of David or menorah in his home. His Russian father spoke with a thick Russian accent, and ran the front of the office and daily business routine. Alex was the only researcher, other than me, in the lab. There was also a Mexican guy from Merida named George with two other laborers in the warehouse. My work freed Alex to spend more time with business projects and on his midnight poetry and philosophy reading. I set my own schedule and worked hard, coming in and out at any time I wished, day or night. Once a week, I turned in my time card—and not once did he ever question it, nor did he have reason to.

I had a large, air-conditioned lab with twenty-four-hour access, so I often used it to study for exams and other work. The lights were bright and there was a large table against the wall with shelves crammed with reagents and samples of all kinds. My favorite place to sit was a long desk, which I covered daily with a clean sheet of paper from a roll attached to the end. It was pure delight to do my calculations and read and write directly on the desktop until I was fully organized for serious studies, tests, and class presentations. I often worked deep into the night. Alex often came in around midnight to read, and after saying hello, disappeared into his office to read more . . . The room was well ventilated to handle the toxic fumes of benzene, acetone, and other solvents and reagents used in the polymerization process for industrial glues. Alex was becoming the major supplier of acrylic glue to the US air force, which had strict detailed specifications for strength and composition. The compounds we developed and tested set the standards of the time and probably exist to the current days. Alex asked me to work as much as I felt capable, always aware that my studies were important.

I commuted on my trusty five-dollar bicycle and in a few months and finally had the money to buy a new Vespa motorcycle for $300. It was exciting to own a real vehicle; and I rode it a lot over the next two years, even up to Aptos to visit the Silverthornes, sometimes to San Francisco, or Sebastopol, as well as the greater LA freeways. He also sent me out to other laboratories to bring their products in his car, while even cheaper personnel were available; he was training me to drive a car. A few months later, Alex asked me to try my Vespa in exchange with his car overnight. He said he liked the fresh air on his face on the ride home to San Pedro and offered me his Oldsmobile sedan as an even exchange. I was making good money then and could afford the insurance, and happily accepted the trade. I clearly got the better end of the deal, but Alex insisted—his way of being generous, perhaps knowing I might refuse an outright gift. I think he really wanted to protect me from the danger of riding the Vespa on the highways, as I never saw him ride the Vespa (motor scooter). He bought a new car soon after.

Chapter Sixteen

Among the Migrant Ministry

By early 1959, Mr. Silverthorne approached me to persuade me to register with the Methodist Conference as a preministerial major. He and Dr. Black had met at the quadrennial conference a month previous and offered support for a scholarship to Claremont Theological Seminary (Methodist) upon my graduation from college. I agreed, thinking I might go to Africa where the most help is needed, like my hero, Albert Schweitzer. By April, I received a letter of invitation to join the California Migrant Ministry. The brochure described a meeting of 150 college students in Fresno for a weeklong training on how to be a good Christian Samaritan to migrant families on the farms and orchards of the San Joaquin Valley. I was again excited to meet Christian colleagues my own age in a stimulating week of day and evening workshops. We were divided into twenty teams consisting of five members each and dispersed to all corners of California farmland to assist in health, education, and the Christian spirit of charity.

We were given a car and an expense account and a salary of $100 a month each. My five-member team was dispatched to Sebastopol, living in the basement of the Sebastopol Methodist Church at the center of town. Our leader, Beverly, was an older second-year theological seminarian; Margaret was a sociology student from the University of Iowa; and Jim Hunter was a potential seminarian, the son of a minister from Indianapolis and two devout young Christian women from the South. Jim Hunter and I set up sleeping quarters on the stage of the auditorium behind the curtains, where we would have many late nightlong conversations each night next two months. The women set up downstairs, which was more secluded and had better accommodations. Since the kitchen and dining area was on the other end of the auditorium, I could hear many other late conversations on intellectual and religious from our colleagues as well.

The next two months were among the most illuminating of my life, as I was exposed to a host of books and ideas that I never heard in college. Jim introduced me to William James' *Varieties of Religious Experience*. Written at the turn of the century Harvard professor, it described the conversion experiences of many people, as well as other types of transcendent experience. I read it voraciously and talked endlessly about it to Jim and Margaret. Another book that was circulating was Kinsey's *Human Sexuality*, which described a scientific survey of varieties of sex and sexual experience across many social settings. It gave me a whole new perspective on human sexuality, and the uniqueness of each individual human sexual psyche, including my own, something that would assist me later greatly in years of psychiatric practice. Others in our group were strictly Bible oriented, and I discussed theological ideas with them. I could not have known it then, but this was a particularly fertile and significant time in American intellectual history.

Our basic routine was to work five days a week, with Saturdays reserved for individual and group recreational activities. On Sundays, we attended services at Sebastopol Methodist Church and sometimes had supper with newly arrived missionaries. We spent every weekdays in migrant's campsites, going to different fields each to meet the families. It was an eye-opener to see so many white families with several children, from toddlers to teenagers, living in run-down trucks with tents on the sides. I did not encounter any black families, but saw a few Mexicans. We were teaching the importance of clean water, babysitting the children, teaching the kids how to read, and sometimes showing movies of Christian values. We had sports equipment and played basketball, volleyball, and softball with the children and the adults, when they were available. We were missionaries.

Truman was eighteen, as I was, the oldest boy of six kids that left Oklahoma when he was thirteen. The family of five all worked in the fields slept in tent or in the truck. He and I studied English together after their supper. He was strikingly alert, good-looking, blond, and could only read a little and did not know how to write. He needed grammar and I needed to pick up some slang and idiomatic American phrases, which to this day are still elusive to me. In the fields, he earned $3.00 a day, while the younger children earned $1.50 and the experienced adults got $4.00. It was difficult to witness young lives bound in repetitive and isolated labor with little to look forward to. I studied Truman daily and he shared his life stories and family problems with me. We even talked about the possibility of him leaving the fields and going into the service, but he felt he was needed to care for his ailing parents and to raise his younger siblings. Toward the end of the summer, upon our departure, Truman pulled out his prized silver and turquoise bolo tie he had inherited from his grandfather and brought all the way from Oklahoma, saying, "I want you to have this." I was amazed, and we were both silent for a while. I thanked him, but replied, "No, you will need it—and it was your grandfather's." There was no way I was going to take his one valued possession, though I was afraid of insulting him. Saying goodbye to Truman was difficult, and I prayed with my Bible in hand for him to have a promising future.

One Saturday evening, Jim, Margaret, and I drove to a Santa Rosa coffee house for a little recreation and to continue our ever-growing discussions on philosophy, theology, and books. I had heard of beatniks before, but had never seen or listened to them. They were a wild-looking gang of bearded and unkempt rebels that lounged around all night talking subversive politics, esoteric art, and philosophy while drinking strong Turkish coffee. While we were talking about the rapid modernization of the world, a skinny man with a goatee and black turtleneck sweater started a spontaneous rant, speaking in rhyme and wailing on his bongos. Then two young men that were sitting on the pavement started chanting what I am sure was a spontaneous refrain in alternately angry-sounding and angelic tones. When we asked where they were from, they said that they were simply traveling around the country sharing ideas, and "digging the visions" of the people that they encountered. They said that they were staying at churches, sleeping in fields sometimes, and "digging their own divine expression to the world." While I could not directly connect to their worldview—as they seemed to curse all forms of establishment, I was intrigued and almost envious of their freedom and ability to devote their lives to their own sense of expression. A couple of them smelled very bad; but they were at least genuine, if not over idealistic in their honest and willing disposition; and they listened to our stories very attentively.

When Margaret told them we were part of the Migrant Ministry, they said they could "dig that" and even offered to come out to the fields to help. The man who appeared to be the leader of the group, who they called "Cosmo," asked us what we were trying to accomplish. When we said it was to build fellowship and commit to the service of our fellow man, particularly the poor and oppressed migrant farm workers, he yelled, "Dig it! Yeah, yeah, yeah—dig it" over and over and started rapping on his bongos faster and faster while his comrades chanted in a frenzied chorus; and another young man made a spontaneous poem about helping the downtrodden. Jim started to chime in with them a little bit, slapping his thighs in rhythm and chanting their refrain. We talked late into the night; and it was easy for me to conclude that there was something brewing in this country, possibly the seeds of a major social revolution. Margaret agreed and told me that there was a significant and growing body of intelligent and educated people that were choosing not to participate in what they considered a corrupt system. A couple of years later, I thought back on this evening when I watched President Eisenhower, the one-time General I had admired as a boy in Korea as I watched his motorcade pass through our neighborhood Seoul, as he gave a foreboding speech his last day in office, warning the American public of the dangers of the "Military-Industrial Complex." Clearly, the stirrings of discontent were well underway that summer.

One Sunday afternoon, we were invited to a large buffet with all the prestigious locals at a neoclassical Italian-style mansion of a wealthy church patron on forty acres of sculpted apple orchards. The hostess was dynamic; and her husband was a well-known local veterinarian who befriended me and ended up inviting me out the following summer, allowing me to assist in animal surgeries. On my second trip to the mansion, I noticed a Japanese family living at the edge of the apple orchard and had a long conversation with the father, a third generation Japanese-American who had made a comfortable life there with his family for thirty years.

Later that summer, we accepted an invitation to water ski on the Russian River. It was my first and indeed very exciting. Margaret and I were very close to each other. She was an avant-garde type and a sociology major—the daughter of an Iowa City lawyer. We could talk for hours and seemed to complete each other's thoughts at times. My conversations with her were just as educational as my courses at Compton and USC; and through her, I gained deeper insight into the soul and social texture of this country—especially from a woman's perspective. We ended up seeing each other off and on for five years.

On following summer, I revisited the veterinarian family in Sebastopol; my Vespa died on the highway on the way back to Gardena, near Bakersfield. As I was checking out the engine, a pickup truck stopped; and the driver suggested I take the motor scooter on his truck to the next garage. As they worked on my bike, he offered his home several miles away for lunch and rest—and extended the offer for me to stay the night. He gave me a tour of his 2000-acre cotton plantation and told me his complete family history. I ended up staying for three days.

Upon returning to SAI, I was introduced to a visitor, from the city of Mokpo, southwestern corner of Korea. I gave her a guided tour of our orphanage including our milking station where I worked. I suddenly realized that those Korean children who lost parents during the war also needed milk.

Subsequently, months hence I negotiated with Dr. Silverthorne and others to ask for donations of milking cows to be sent to Korea. This Heifer Project was a nonprofit charity organization. In the next several months, we received a half dozen cows and finally found an American Shipping Company, pro bono to ship those cows to Korea. In 1963, when I bid farewell to my dying father, I also went to the orphanage for the milk production, some 200 young orphans lined up on both sides of the road cheering me with songs. I have long relished the donors of the cows and the happy faces of the children.

Chapter Seventeen

Out to Find America

When I started at University of Southern California (USC), I had a twenty-mile freeway commute on my Vespa, a dangerous proposition. I had an urge to leave SAI and found a family to live with through a church where I had spoke on my Migrant Ministry experience, but my daily commute was still too far. Finally, I was introduced by Mr. Howe again to the Walden House, a Methodist (free for me) housing facility a few blocks from campus for university students. I stayed there, but still had to drive scooter down the glue lab two or three times a week. Once I was rescued by my physics professor, Dr. Waddell (who recognized me having earned two consecutive As) by chance when my Vespa broke down on the interstate. I often hitchhiked at the freeway entrances, which was probably illegal.

I took an Introduction to Religious Philosophy course taught by a Methodist minister turned professor, Dr. Robb, from whom I learned about the concept of the "leap of faith" and the theology of Thomas Aquinas. I became more people-oriented, which led to more courses in sociology, physical anthropology, English literature, History of Western Civilization written by the same lecturer, Dr. Wallbank. While I was committed to the path to practicing medicine, I remained compelled by the prospects of having my own ministry in some manner.

Life at USC was even busier than it had been at Compton. When some of the Walden House residents expressed jealousy to the house chaplain because I had a car by then, to commute to work, while still receiving a room-and-board stipend. I knew I would have to find other lodging. I found a small room for $25 a month, even closer to my classes; but cooking was forbidden. I lived off on canned foods. When low in cash, I resorted to dog food; horsemeat tasted best. I also foraged the dumpsters at the supermarkets early in the morning before garbage pick up. My wartime survival skills from the old country were still with me indeed.

The demanding premed curriculum, combined with working at the lab and tending to the rest of life's requirements did often feel like protracted war!

While at Walden House, I had seen a flyer for a unique summer job in New York City on a church bulletin board. The New York City Archdiocese of the Episcopal Church advertised the position of manager of the Chelsea Episcopal Church during a priest's sabbatical for two months of July and August with a $200/month stipend with room and board at the church rectory. Again, the urge to explore America grabbed hold of me. Having confirmed the position by April, I advertised on the student bulletin board to share the costs of driving to New York after graduation. Amir, an Israeli student who wanted to return to Tel Aviv via New York, responded. We met and he inspected the car and agreed to share all costs, including any needed repairs from LA to New York along the southern route. To save time, neither of us attended graduation ceremonies, which meant little to me, other than another transition to medical school.

We packed all our possessions and started out, excited about the adventure. We passed Palms Springs quickly and entered Arizona on a very hot day. The desert red rock formations looked otherworldly, and my companion had never seen Saguaro cacti before. I remembered how Barry had initiated me to the desert a few years ago; and now I was initiating Amir, whose jaw dropped repeatedly upon seeing the great canyons and rock formations across the southwest. We hit Phoenix by dusk, and after checking motel prices decided to stay at a YMCA. We set out early the next morning hoping to make Texas by dusk, but had a tire blowout somewhere in New Mexico. After we got to a town, I found a new tire for $25, but my companion insisted on buying a retread. He ended up paying his half for the new one, but was unhappy about it. At the next town, he got on a Greyhound, citing fear of more expenses as his reason.

Now alone, I wondered if I had enough money to make to New York. Somewhere near El Paso, I got tired, and to save money, decided to sleep in the car. The night was cold and I slept poorly. The next day I made it as far as the oil town of Odessa. Early in the evening, I checked into the Salvation Army transient lodging for three dollars, which included morning breakfast. I shared a room with three older, tough-looking men. Though I was trembling with fear inside, I decided this was not a place to show weakness and engaged them in conversation during breakfast to evaluate my position. They were planning to work as day hands in the oil fields that day. I decided to join them and went to the labor office at 8 a.m. to find a day's work and bolster my stores for the long journey still ahead. It was a good opportunity to learn about this new part of the country. We rode on an open-truck bed across parched grasslands to transport equipment and furniture to an oil field facility. It was hard work, but I made $15 in cash.

That evening I stumbled upon a local tavern to experience working class Odessa. A burly patron was shooting pool and invited me to play. I declined, as

I. DAVID HONG MD, US NAVY CAPTAIN, RETIRED

I did want telling him I was broke and trying to get to New York. I was afraid I might be a target for some kind of heist; but he bought me a beer and I shot pool with him anyway—the first time I had ever played. Later he showed me pictures of naked women in vulgar positions and spoke with great pride of various sexual conquests. I encouraged him to talk so that I could learn about this segment of society. Others joined us, one who had just gotten out of jail and was running from the police. I suspected that they all were carrying concealed weapons. Indeed, I was in the Wild West that I had watched in countless American movies as a boy in Korea, fascinated by the rugged, whiskey-drinking characters waiting for an excuse to fight. I thought that some of those characters must have been derived from some of these ruffians from Odessa.

After another good night's rest and breakfast for three dollars, I left early in the morning toward Dallas on a long, lonely drive across more empty sagebrush land. Somewhere near Abilene, I saw a man with a duffel bag standing on the side of the road and picked him up out of boredom. I told him where I was going and that I was running out of money and needed someone to share gas expenses. He was headed north for cooler weather and driving wheat combines for day wages, as he had done for the past several years. The more I talked about our actual lives, the more detached and uncomfortable I became, as he clearly could not relate to me. I countered this by unloading fictitious troubles on him, including fabricated run-ins with the police to keep him on guard, as I was growing increasingly suspicious of him. I even stole some of the stories from the guys I had worked with in Odessa, such as having to punch out a cop who pulled me over in order to make a getaway. He was on the run from the police and that is why he was looking for day wages only, so as to remain invisible. I grew more fearful as he recounted some of his crimes, and I was certain he had a weapon on him. I played his game, sympathizing with him that I was in a similar predicament with the law, to keep him appeased in some strange manner. I was scared to death of him and worried he might steal the car, or worse. I pulled into a small gas station/market and left the keys in the car to show that I trusted him, or that he could run away with the car, as I thought that this would be better than a physical encounter on the isolated highways ahead. When I returned, he agreed to share half the gas money; and we were both more at ease with each other, driving east and sharing expenses all the way. I left him on a northbound highway to Kansas and spent another night in a Salvation Army shelter somewhere on the hot dusty plains.

I started east the next day for Shreveport, which looked like a large, busy town on the map. It got even hotter and very humid as I went through Louisiana. I drove through the white section of town into the black neighborhoods, which I wanted to experience. I needed a haircut and entered a black barbershop to study the people. Two young men in their late '20s ran the place, which also seemed to be a social nexus for an extended group of friends, including several women, their girlfriends I supposed. They were naturally very curious about me, as they had never seen an Asian before, and asked if I was Japanese. I said yes, as I almost always did to such questions to avoid needless talk about Korea, or Japan for that matter, about which, no doubt, they knew little.

After a haircut with a tip, I inquired into the possibility of sleeping with a local family for student prices. The young barber, Jimmy, managed to find me a room with a family for three days for $10. In the evening, he invited me to join his friends for a pork barbeque and then to the armory for dancing. He was protective of me and eager to show off his new guest in town. By 9 p.m., we arrived at a large brick building, a Civil War armory with high ceilings and wooden floors reminiscent of a turn-of-the-century fancy bar in the black section of Shreveport. Some one hundred or more attended, dancing into a sweaty frenzy to a loud sound system playing rock and roll and rhythm and blues. There was a large window and ceiling fan that ventilated the place well. The room was filled with a cacophony of elated squeals, uproarious laughter, and wild dancing for hours. I had never seen such unbridled expression of body movement. The deep, soulful music and pulsing rhythm animated the frenzied crowd; and I could feel the body heat funneling out of the building when I stood outside. I felt almost jealous at their unrestrained freedom while my own life seemed so bound with worry.

Jimmy invited me back and asked for my New York phone number, since he had some relatives there and wanted to come up to see me. It seemed that blacks led much more carefree lives than whites did, with true abundance, not in the sense of money, but an environment that offered unlimited easy fishing in the creeks and vegetables that grew all year around with little care. The highway on both sides was covered with growth and vines, the land was rich and fishes were jumping in the water. It seemed that nearly everybody had a car, but usually old jalopies. There seemed to be no danger or potential violence, and no need for discipline or restraints in their social life. Everybody was equal and treated each other in a friendly manner—men and women together, poor in cash assets but happy. Now I knew I had felt Louisiana on my skin; and the thick magnolia scent in the air, along with the indescribable floral medleys that came from the steamy swamps and slow moving rivers stayed with me all the way to New York. I knew I had caught the essence of these beautiful people, and the land that held them stayed in my memory forever. I will never forget the big white smiles across those black faces, and how they welcomed me into their community, even if for just a couple of days.

The next day, there were many hitchhikers; but I did not pick any up because I wanted to be alone and contemplate my journey to this point. I passed through small towns, stopping briefly for lunch and canned foods. My goal was to cross the Mighty Mississippi River and start looking for a place to rest for a day. I saw signs for Millsap College, a small private school near Vicksburg whose famous

I. DAVID HONG MD, US NAVY CAPTAIN, RETIRED

Civil War battle I had studied in American history class. It was a historical early plantation settlement on the shores of the Mississippi, the true heart of the deep South. I visited the students on the campus during their summer session and was invited to stay in the dormitory, which had an abundance of empty rooms and a cafeteria nearby. It was a good deal; and after a restful day, I departed the next morning, since I was only halfway to New York.

I arrived in Jackson, Mississippi, in the early evening looking for another Salvation Army transient shelter. I decided to tour the nearby Jackson Methodist Church, a handsome classic brick building. Inside I found several college students in the middle of a discussion group and was welcomed to participate in a spiritual discussion. The meeting ended at about ten in the evening. They must have talked to each other about my plans to stay at the Salvation Army nearby, because somehow Dr. Roy Clark, pastor of the church, approached me and invited me to stay with his family overnight. He was a tall, statuesque man born in the south and educated at Yale Divinity School, where I intended to visit, along with Harvard during my stay in New York. He lived with his devoted wife and two young daughters in a style of Southern gentility.

By the time I reached beautiful Nashville and then north toward Pennsylvania without a mishap, I felt confident that I would arrive in New York on schedule. I continued to sleep at Salvation Armies or in the car along the way, or sometimes I made friends who would put me up. There were some Freedom Riders along the way—Nashville college kids, both black and white protesting for Civil Rights and challenging Jim Crow laws throughout the South. During this summer, there were a lot of problems and scenes, sometimes violent, throughout the South regarding segregation and other issues. Acts of civil disobedience were occurring everywhere. At the time, I could have no idea how historically important these events were, or that I had witnessed America at such a pivotal time. The country I was becoming part of was changing before my eyes in ways that I could only understand later.

The green rolling hills of Nashville and the traditional colonial homes and running creeks nearby and Belle Mead with beautiful Greek styled mansions made a deep impression on me. In fact, I had almost premonitory sensations that would make sense much later. My heart felt at ease there, and I noticed a calming sense of belonging somehow connected to the smell of the air specially when I saw the replica of Parthenon in Greece. Even the flora of the area struck familiar chords inside me. I knew I would be back there in some capacity, but did not know what for.

I then drove on toward Philadelphia through Amish farm country and found a lone, bearded farmer hauling hay on a horse cart. I needed lodging and some food and was curious about his community. I introduced myself as a church worker on the way to New York and offered labor in return for a lodging on his haystack. I showed him my letter inviting me to the Episcopal Church in New York, and he smiled and heartily invited me to his farm. We worked together well; and by evening, he offered me the extra room in his house for the night, after a delicious dinner with his family. This was the most elaborate meal I have ever seen, and their fresh raw butter and milk with the cream still on top was the sweetest I have ever tasted.

    I arrived at the Chelsea Episcopal Church at Ninth Ave. and Thirty-fourth St. and met Bishop McEvoy who oversaw all of the Episcopal Churches in New York. We went to his central office in a Manhattan high-rise, owned by the church. He then opened an account at a nearby Jewish grocery store where I could order all of my food while living in the second floor rectory behind the main altar. It had air-conditioning and a full kitchen. I was introduced to a janitor and given a key to the front door. Bishop McEvoy explained that the regular priest was in Italy and would be back on August 15. The church was officially closed since communion was not possible; but there was a lot of demand by the parishioners to open the church for prayer, especially on Sundays. With my help, the congregation organized an informal prayer session; and others prayed individually in the Church. It took about a week to get to know the names of all the parishioners.

    One evening there was an urgent knock on the door by a young Cuban named Miguel who asked me to open up so he could play the organ, which he was used to doing. I had seen him before, so I obliged and he sat at the organ and played a Bach fugue in G minor from memory at full volume. He then played other Renaissance music, which enthralled me because I used to listen to Albert Schweitzer playing similar music on his organ, presumably in the jungles of Africa, surrounded by Swedish nurses in LIFE magazine in 1958 and imagined myself doing the same. We soon became friends. It was not clear to me what kind of job he had; only that he considered himself an artist and lived four blocks south near Greenwich Village. Miguel had rafted over the Caribbean as a refugee by himself to seek asylum in America. He later told me about his several days at sea and how he was sick and dehydrated, certain that he would die. He prepared some delicious Cuban meals for me in his dilapidated fourth-floor walk-up studio. His nightly playing became a ritual of meditation and comfort for me as I contemplated my life and relationship to God, accompanied his beautiful songs, then locking the door when he left. It occurred to me that there were others who had sacrificed and risked much more than I, and succeeded with far less support, having even fewer resources and possessions in order to become an American. I felt how truly fortunate I was and took Miguel's teachings in this regard to heart and felt that we were brothers in some way.

    I had a lot of time during the day and kept my car parked on the street, occasionally driving it; but I seldom needed it in New York. I met an elderly

I. DAVID HONG MD, US NAVY CAPTAIN, RETIRED

English theologian, Emily, living at the seminary on Ninth Ave., only two blocks from the Chelsea Church. She invited me for three o'clock tea at her home on the compound, which had dozens of charming apartments. Emily introduced me to her daughter, Ann of same age; and the three of us had many discussions about adapting to America, and most of all a book called *The Natural Superiority of Women* by Ashley Montague in which the author expounded on the physical, social, mental, and emotional superiority of the female sex. She also served afternoon teas. I had never heard such ideas before and was intrigued as it defied all the notions of women I had learned in my upbringing in Korea, and asserted that the historical subjugation of women by men has been at the heart of our worst societal problems and had possibly hampered civilization itself. However, wise men knew on some level that they were inferior to them, even if it was only by virtue of the fact that women could produce human beings and men could not, and that men subconsciously knew they were essentially expendable and reacted with hostility, dominating women with their physical strength. This is how I was introduced to the women's movement. Ann and I went out for a long drive; and we had a detailed discussion about the book; but I did not find her attractive somehow, even though she stimulated me intellectually. We found ourselves in opposition on many scores, including what I thought was her tendency to demonize all men as a function of her own personal anger. My mind was still fixed on Margaret from the Migrant Ministry who also had a job in New York at the time and was living with a black family in Harlem doing social work in the ghetto.

Father McEvoy was pleased with how I was managing the church, and every two weeks came by and took me to lunch to review matters. In mid-August, I was invited to the reception party of the returning priest of Chelsea Episcopal. I was given a printed invitation with directions, and could not believe where the map took me—through Hudson Parkway along a beautiful drive and up a winding driveway to an amazing three-story brick house with a slate roof and granite porch and a driveway overlooking the Hudson River, with manicured boxwood shrub borders. The house was filled with Chinese antiques that her grandfather had brought home from China after the Boxer's Rebellion in the 1880s. The lovely matron of the mansion recommended a summer drink. Noting my hesitation at the options, she offered me my first gin and tonic with lime, which I liked very much—my first real drink, and one that I've cherished ever since. I saw that the eastern US is very different from the west in that established families and traditions were more important.

As planned, at the end of August, I picked up Margaret in Poughkeepsie; and we took a leisurely drive to Niagara Falls and finally back to her family in Iowa City, where I spent three nights. I then drove alone all the way back to California via the northern route, reflecting on the past three months and got ready to apply to medical school.

Chapter Eighteen

My First Return to Korea: Rediscovering the Stories

My plan was to impose myself on SAI again where I was always welcome and knew many people—unless I could find a cheap place near USC. It is almost ironic that my car would not start the day after I got back from my trip. Initially I was able to push-start it, but it soon completely died. I salvaged it and found another cheap used car and got another small room for $25 a month. I still had a long commute to work.

I got a message from Mr. Howe from SAI that a family was looking for someone like me to support through college and he had been saving their name and number for me all summer. I went to see the Putnams who lived in Bell, not far from campus. "Uncle Ben" and "Aunt Merle," as I would come to call them, was a childless couple in their '50s with an extra room, wishing to provide a home for a poor student like me. She immediately took a liking to me and told me the saga of their early years in the 1930s when he was about nineteen and had to leave home to find work because of the poverty during depression in rural California. Aunt Merle ran a boarding house, which she later inherited; and Ben came there to board. She was three years older than him, unmarried, not having found a suitable man until Ben came along. Ben was hardworking, well mannered, and had a twinkle in his eye. She would shower him with extra delectables that she made just for him when he returned each night from heavy construction work. They fell in love and lived in the boarding house until they saved enough to buy their present home. He was playful with her while she worried needlessly about him, as she soon would for me. Ben went to the South Pacific with the Navy, returned home to Aunt Merle, and they were even closer than before. After taking a course in drawing blueprints for apartments and houses, Ben started venturing out to buy empty

I. DAVID HONG MD, US NAVY CAPTAIN, RETIRED

land with Aunt Merle's boarding house money and built post-war duplexes and other properties.

She was a natural cook; and he was an efficient worker, leaving home every morning with his pickup and a last cup of coffee on the way to meet his crew. He showed me the blueprints of an apartment complex he had started.

Every Sunday he pulled his blue Cadillac out of the garage, and we went for a long drive in the cushy air-conditioned car. I had a spacious bedroom across from the living room with a separate bath, which Aunt Merle volunteered to clean, just as she had done when she ran the boarding house. A few months later in November, she was disturbed to find Karl Marx's *Communist Manifesto* in my room. It was required reading for the sociology course I was taking. America was still in the aftereffects of the Red Scare, and she was a sympathizer to McCarthy's inquisition with the Un-American Activities Committee. Though she remained suspicious, she accepted my explanation of required reading sociology class.

The highlight of my semester was when I invited them to attend my opera class's opening night performance of Stravinsky's *Rake's Progress,* in which I played a minor role and was a member of the chorus. They arrived in the Cadillac; and after the show came down to the stage to greet me and the other performers, including the leading vocalist who had suddenly froze and became aphonic, due to stress, I think. The event was one of the most exciting that they had ever attended, even though they had a hard time following the play.

In September, as soon as I was settled into Ben and Aunt Merle's, I confidently applied to only three medical schools to save on application fees: Harvard, Yale, and Johns Hopkins. I never thought about applying to cheaper, easier state universities. By March, I received rejection letters from all three. I was amazed, since I had scarcely failed at anything since arriving in the US. I was humbled and took some time to mull things over, lick my wounds, and confer with Ben and Merle who were always there to console me. Aunt Merle encouraged me to try again and promised that she would give me $200 a month throughout the four years of medical school if I was accepted the next year, which she indeed fulfilled. With her encouragement, I reapplied to twice as many medical schools the following September and retook the MCAT exam after studying more. I also concentrated on second-tier schools, including USC, Marquette, Vanderbilt, University of Edinburgh in Scotland, and Rochester. By March of the following year, they had all accepted me.

At about that same time, I received news that my father had severe emphysema and could not walk more than half a block due to shortness of breath. He said he wanted to see me before it was too late, but did not have the money to pay for my trip. Since I had graduated and had a one-year hiatus before starting medical school, I planned to earn enough money to get back to Korea for the first time in seven years. I hoped to arrange cheap passage on the return trip through India,

Europe, England, and New York, and then back to any medical school with acceptance. Since I had a BA cum laude, it was easy to find a job. For a while, I was a biologist in a tuna processing plant in Long Beach. The job was fun, but dealing with seaman was not very stimulating; and the drive from Bell was thirty miles each way, so I let it go. My second job was near Bell at an industrial marine paint company, which used zinc oxide as a base to reduce rusting on hull, oxidation of metal, on large commercial and military vessels. There were a dozen research technicians working on their popular "Americoat" product.

I decided to go to Vanderbilt for medical school while I was on this job. The timing was perfect; and I gave notice and bought a one-way air ticket to Seoul, via Hawaii and Tokyo, my first time on an airplane, a Boeing 707.

My mother met me at the airport in her sedan, and we were driven to the hospital in-house nurses' quarters. I settled in her suite to stay a while and got caught up on what had happened the past seven years. In the evening, I saw my ailing father who still lived in the once-proud, now-dilapidated house where I was born. The house had been extended to accommodate two more families for rents, and it was in bad shape. I stayed mostly with my mother, since she had a modern bathroom and used chairs instead of traditional floor living. I could no longer sit on the floor more than a few minutes. I also met my father's four-year-old son, Jun-Pyo and his second wife. Dad complimented me on my graduation and for getting home on my own. He had heard that many of his friends' kids were having much more difficulty in America than I was, and said that he knew I would succeed from the start. When I asked him how he knew, he replied simply, "I trusted you." That was the end of our conversation about America because he knew little about it except for what he and I experienced through American soldiers during the war. He maintained his livelihood through leasing his home, but did not have any extra money or assets, since he sold the other properties for my education a few years ago, and had long ago conceded most of the shared assets to my mother.

I discussed my father's condition with his doctors and proposed a new evaluation and treatment, since I knew I could get considerable cash from my mother with a little coaxing. In the following weeks, while staying in her suite, I discovered that she was holding about $1,000,000 in stocks and other real estate she had acquired since her return to Korea in 1953. It was difficult to understand how a mother of such wealth had nothing to contribute toward my education, nor to any of her three children, for that matter. She did contribute only half of the college tuition to my sisters in Korea, and none after they arrived in the US. I talked her into giving me $3,000 to help my father. Not even doctors trusted checks then in Korea, so I had to bring the money to the hospital in a bag.

I took Dad in taxis out for courtyard dining for a few times and one evening rented a gazebo at the Buddhist temple, something he loved immensely. He adamantly thought I should marry a Korean girl and introduced his friend, the head of the Pharmacy Department at the Seoul Medical University to discuss the marriage of his daughter. I took her out and liked her, but could not seriously consider marriage at the age of 22, not to mention the problem of a Korean girl's acculturation to the US. My father agreed that I was a little too young, but questioned me with urgency, "If not now, how will you find a Korean girl! How can you live without the support of a good woman?" On the second score, I think he was right. I would be very busy in medical school, and Nashville would run me ragged.

My older sister, Nami, came to Los Angeles and was working in as a nurse at Kaiser Hospital on Sunset Boulevard. She was tall, beautiful, charming, and liked to be flirted, a sort of femme fatal. She got everything out of my mother in terms of money, and was provided the finest clothes and accessories. There were always young men salivating around her, and she relished being courted.

My youngest sister, Julie, had been living with my dying father and stepmother all this time. She would sob when I approached her, and was quite needy of my attention. She got nothing out of my mother in terms of financial or emotional support, or from our dying father and stepmother with five-year-old boy in tow. She had always been the neglected one, and was somewhat homely. I think she suffered the most of all the children, and never really got to know our mother. I gave considerable cash to her often, and she was always tearfully thankful. Our sick father and stepmother neglected Julie. Still she felt helpless watching him weaken over the course of those months. She wanted to find some way to magically cure him, and I think would have done anything if she had the means, but they were getting poorer every year. It reminded me of this traditional Korean folk tale that my aunt told me this way a long time ago:

> "Sim-Chung was raised by her widowed father who loved her dearly. He was blind, and when Sim-Chung became a young woman, she wanted to heal his blindness. After asking around all the neighboring villages, she heard of a special healer who could restore her father's sight using ancient herbs and special chants to the gods, but the charge would be 300 pounds of rice, an amount impossible for her to get.
>
> "As she was wandering about the villages looking for help for her father, she had heard that one village had an important ceremony each year where they threw a young maiden into the river to become the River God's wife. Of course, the villagers did not wish to sacrifice their own daughters to the river, so they customarily looked for a girl from another village. Sim-Chung told the village leaders that if they gave 300 pounds of rice to the healer so he would cure his father that she would sacrifice herself to be the River God's wife. They agreed and all the villagers gathered around her, sang,

waved banners, and made offerings as she made this ultimate sacrifice and leapt into the river.

"There was a crow in a pine tree near the river watching this ceremony, and as Sim-Chung dove into the water, their eyes met, and the crow immediately took flight to her father's little house in the next village and told him what had happened. The crow spoke in perfect Korean to the father about what had just transpired and then led the blind old man all the way to the river. As the crow told the details of how brave Sim-Chung was, and how beautiful she looked, garlanded in flowers and dressed in silk, the old man wailed and wept so hard and uncontrollably that two crystals fell out of his eyes into the water. He yelled again and again, 'Sim-Chung, my beloved daughter, how I will miss you!'

"He wept for hours as the crow stood over him in the pine branch above. The crow whispered to the old man, 'Open your eyes, my poor friend and look upon this holy river where your daughter made such a brave sacrifice.'

"As the old man opened his eyes, he was speechless as he could suddenly see with great intensity all the colors of creation and wept again for the beauty of it, though he was still heartbroken and said, 'Yes the river is beautiful, but what good is this beauty if I cannot see it with my beloved daughter?'

"He continued to weep and suddenly, from the crystals that had been flushed from his eyes, he saw a water lily sprout from river in a matter of seconds. He could not believe his now-seeing eyes. And from the beautiful, freshly opened lavender blossom of the lily emerged the body of his daughter, still alive and as beautiful as ever, singing an enchanting river song that made all the villagers weep for its perfection. Sim-Chung was alive and well and walked to her father and embraced him and they wept in joy together. The villagers brought the ten large bags of rice and other food and valuables down to the river and gave them to the father and his daughter, and they returned home with plenty of food for the coming winter and their hearts full of immense gratitude and happiness."

There was one young man among several that were always milling around trying to gain my mother's attention and befriend Nami. He showered my mother and me with gifts and cakes almost a week. Mother would accept the gifts and donate them to her favorite charities. These young aspiring sons-in-law were very aggressive and resourceful, and even found my address in America and later began sending unwanted gifts in Nashville. One of the suitors measured my shoe size from a footprint and sent hand-made shoes to me in America, though they did not fit and were too heavy. Eventually, some years later, Nami married one of those suitors with Mother's blessing. The marriages failed quickly; and there was abuse done to my sister, as Mother did not deliver the expected dowries. She was

I. DAVID HONG MD, US NAVY CAPTAIN, RETIRED

one of the richest and most powerful women then in Korea, yet continually failed in providing expected financial support for education and support her children, and ultimately injuring her family name.

I heard Uncle Ilhan; Mother's brother was in Seoul and called him to have lunch at the fashionable Bando Hotel where he had been living right across from the old US embassy. It was the fourth and last time I would meet Ilhan. We discussed my future plans to travel the world before starting medical school in the fall. He was pleased and volunteered to write letters to his trading partners in Holland and Italy, where three months later, I was royally entertained with all expenses paid in both countries. In Korea, I also toured one of his orphanage/vocational schools where a few hundred boys were raised and trained in various technologies. I donated $200 out of my pocket to the orphanage. Uncle Ilhan ended up leaving most of his assets to Yonsei University—about $30,000,000 at the time of his death. Almost all Koreans today still know his name. I have wondered at the meaning of this large donation to an educational institution, since he failed to contribute to the education of his two dozen very poor nephews and nieces, several of them orphans after the war. Still, he told me he was very proud of me.

During that stay in Korea, I took a trip to the east to a resort village called Kang-Leung with another eager-to-please sister Naomi's suitor. After a three-day trip by rail, bus taxi, and jeep, we arrived at the foothills of Surak Mountain, known as the most beautiful in all of Korea and were told a legend of this mountain by a local innkeeper.

> *"Once there was a logger who lived alone on this mountain. One day while chasing a deer with his bow and arrow, he came upon a thundering waterfall cascading down into the misty lake far below. Suddenly he saw four magnificent goddess-angels with radiant beams of light emanating from their heads descend from the heavens in a big bucket attached by a golden rope. The vessel was lowered below the mists of the lake while the logger, in a lustful state crawled on all fours to watch the voluptuous angels take off their clothes and bathe. He snuck through the forest and skillfully hid the clothes of the one he favored. Hours later, the heavenly chariot came down again to take the angels back, but the one without clothes could not go, and had to be left behind. The logger then slowly approached her and proclaimed his love as he returned her clothes. They eventually married, but she had to renounce her angel status and become human in order to be the logger's bride."*

We stayed at a local inn, where the hostess served us dinner. In the morning, we had hearty breakfasts before the six-hour climb up to the ancient Buddhist monastery near the summit. The innkeeper told us we might see a recent convert who lives there as a nun, and who was apparently already legendary. She told the story:

> "Three years ago, on one fine Saturday morning in the early summer, a lone beautiful young woman in a fancy American blue dress with high heels and a dressy hat started climbing the mountain and disappeared behind a large boulder. The townsfolk were very curious and concerned since it appeared impossible for her to make the climb so unprepared. Stirred by this unusual spectacle, an old woman followed her from a distance. The young lady noticed and hastened her pace, taking on the rugged boulder-strewn road, crossing knee-deep rushing streams where few dared to tread. Along the way, the young lady threw away the heavy bag she was carrying. After another hour of climbing, she discarded her coat, and then her new hat, and continued up the winding path through the misty pines, curiously still in her shiny blue pumps. The young woman had been climbing three hours as the old woman watched in the distance, following even more suspiciously for two more hours. The young lady came upon a large granite boulder above a cataract and sat in Buddhist meditation staring straight down at the stream, motionless in deep contemplation. Finally, the worried old woman caught up with her and approached. The young woman was feverishly writing a suicide note, which the older woman surmised, as she had seen many suicides there over the years. She started comforting the young woman, suggesting that she give up her earthly desires as the Buddha had done—and as she too had done in her younger years. The older woman then guided her higher and higher up the mountain until they arrived at the temple, which was built hundreds of years earlier. The young woman reclaimed her life as a devout nun and works and meditates at the temple to this day . . ."

We had the same destination for the afternoon as the two nuns in the story, and after hearing the tale, were more energized to climb, half hoping to encounter the legendary nun. We climbed between the massive boulders and pines, across many rushing streams to a particularly large granite boulder on a flat ledge. The vegetation thinned as we climbed. Whenever we saw a large boulder with a cliff, we wondered if it was the one where the young soon-to-be nun had pondered her fate. After six hours of climbing, we saw the curving cornices of a traditional tiled roof where we hoped to see this woman who had exchanged her earthly desires for the pursuit of enlightenment through a monastic life. Upon entering the outer perimeter gate, it is customary to donate money, which we did generously, and then requested lunch since we had not eaten for several hours of hard climbing. After half an hour of sitting and reading a Buddhist text and observing the temple

I. DAVID HONG MD, US NAVY CAPTAIN, RETIRED

artifacts, a meal was brought to us by a nun in traditional Buddhist attire. As she was about to leave, I asked how long she had been at this temple. She politely said three years and disappeared gracefully without engaging us further. I am fairly certain she was the woman from the story.

There are so many stories that were critical in helping me gauge my own life and find sympathy for my fellow man, even across great reaches of time. When I was fifteen, while waiting for visa, I had shed many tears reading Goethe's *The Sorrows of Young Werther,* in Korean translation. It was the story of an unhappy love affair between Goethe himself and his best friend's fiancé, over which young Werther kills him with a pistol. I thought of Margaret for some reason and how I loved her, but she was too distant, cold, and hyper-intellectual, while I needed a more traditional woman. Our love was symbolically killed somehow on this trip, and without a sound. I am not sure how I knew it was over, other than I was renewing myself through this return to my origins and trip around the globe.

When I came back from Korea, I was ready to proceed with the next leg of my journey, after London and New York. I booked a cruise ship with the cheapest possible fare. The travel agency at the Bando Hotel got me a student fare, in a four-in-one cabin with bunk beds. The S S Arcadia had been part of an old British Pacific and Orient steamship company going back 200 years. I also booked a one-way flight to Hong Kong, where I was to board. I stayed two nights in Hong Kong and explored the museums and pagodas among the masses of people. I did not feel comfortable in the dusty, noisy throngs so overrun by commerce, general panic, and maddened crowds.

The Arcadia was comfortable, clean, and cool, with great dinners served in full formal English fashion by an Indian crew. I encountered a Pakistani with seven wives who was always at the same table dressed in traditional garb. They did not converse at all, but managed to communicate in other ways. I wondered what they did between meals, since I never saw any of them mulling about in the open, or on the deck during the entire cruise.

On the cruise, there was a self-proclaimed Turkish Count named George Costello with his English wife, Lady Patricia, whom he treated almost like a child. She was skinny and pale, and in retrospect, I suspected she had neurasthenic symptoms. He treated her like a china doll. She was entirely dependent on him and always in a supine position and very anemic looking. George was intellectually vibrant, trained in classical and pre-Socratic philosophy. I visited him later in their home at the Cumberland hotel in London where they lived after I disembarked from the ship in Naples.

The Arcadia's first stop was Manila. I fled the unsafe and crowded city for the countryside, saw some cock fights, and ate several mangos. After that we stopped in Singapore which had the most memorable botanical gardens I have ever seen—especially the rare orchids which I would revisit years later. Bombay was a revelation, with its poverty, masses of people and beggars, though I loved the impressive colonial era structures and ancient structures in the city. In Arden (now Yemen), we refueled and I got to venture into a Muslim Market where they sold a lot of gold accessories and ornate daggers, some of which I got to handle. In Alexandria, I saw the site of the rebuilt great library that burned down, then took a tour of the Pyramids, rode a camel to the Great Pyramid of Giza, and crawled all the way to the center through a narrow tunnel where the Pharos's sarcophagus had been robbed. I finally disembarked from the Arcadia at Naples with only a light bag, having arranged to pick up the rest of my stuff later in London. I spent six more weeks hitchhiking and staying at hostels across Europe, visiting Rome, Florence, Salzburg, Vienna, Munich, Paris, up to Denmark, Oslo, and over to the British Isles before I flew out from London.

In New York, I made hasty phone calls to local hostels and got a round trip Greyhound ticket to LA in anticipation of my return to Nashville, where I would settle into medical school. After two days on the bus, still enthralled by the American countryside and glad to have returned to my true homeland, I arrived in LA and rejoined Aunt Merle and Uncle Ben, who were glad to see me after six months. I felt like I had undergone yet another rite of passage on the trip, and re-gathered a piece of my soul through the time spent in Korea. I was fairly sure that it would be the last time I would see my father, though I was still hoping for the best.

CHAPTER NINETEEN

Vanderbilt Medical School

In early September 1963, I finally arrived at the McIntyre student dormitory at Vanderbilt, where most of the first-year medical students from out of town lived two to a room. My roommate, Bill from Louisville, was a fine Christian gentleman who eventually became an orthopedic professor. Altogether, there were fifty-two medical freshmen from forty states, all white Americans except me.

I tried hard every day to establish myself in the medical school community just as I had at Glendale High and Compton College. All of us were shocked at the rigors of the program, especially after the anatomical cadaver dissection. Two students had already dropped out by this point. I studied hard to stay in the top third of the class, as we were continually ranked at either the top, middle, or bottom third. The first year was the most difficult with all the core classes in biochemistry, anatomy, and physiology. At the end of the year, I was so tired, like all the others that I decided to do something totally different for the summer by living on a farm and riding, cleaning, and training horses. I worked in a stable outside of Louisville and lived on bread, water, and vegetables, sleeping on the haystack in the barn. After my work was done, I would ride horses to my heart's content through the wild hills of Kentucky, sometimes finding myself in isolated little hamlets, too small to be on a map. I often got lost and became very anxious, but discovered that the horse always knows the way back, and by sunset always found the way home. I did not realize that horses had this kind of sense. I don't think I've ever felt as free as when riding a fast stallion through those forested hills, crossing little sparkling creeks and eyeing the horizon through the high clearings.

At the beginning of the second year, I decided to move out of the dormitory to save money and found a cheaper more pleasant lodging with a classmate, Tom Fulghum. He was born and bred for generations in Atlanta. Where I would visit a couple of times to his magnificent antebellum house on a beautiful creek. Tom's parents had a ski boat, which we took out on many lakes that year waterskiing and partying with his high school friends, and sometimes fishing and camping on the shores in Atlanta.

During second year, I had an almost visionary or paranormal experience after spending many hours studying cellular structures through slides under the microscope for pathology class. I experienced a profound, almost disturbing illusion of seeing cellular structures and blood vessels as cobblestone roads with houses on both sides, leading to myriad networks of consciousness. I then saw myself as a microscopic particle traveling across these blood vessel roads to small villages surrounded by old houses in rural Italian village I visited—all under a microscope. As I visited these houses, molecules would come out to greet me and impart great volumes of information to me, almost like massive computer downloads; only this was well before the first available computer. After looking at this consciousness/blood traffic phenomenon, I realized my interest in how human interactions are realized in human pathology and behavior. It was a fully lucid waking dream, where for a few minutes, I felt like I had access to understanding almost anything. Years later when I shared this story with a colleague who had studied metaphysics, he told me I had experienced what he called "cosmic consciousness." I reread and reflected on William James' *Varieties of Religious Experience* that had made such an impact that summer living in Sebastopol Migrant Ministry.

My second year summer job was with the department of psychiatry where I met Dr. Cromwell who was studying physiological variables in image perception measured in fractions of seconds with an electronic monitoring system. The project grant took me to a Boston state mental hospital where I spent four weeks gathering data on the physiological reaction time of chronically ill schizophrenic patients at the same hospital where Freud worked when he first came to the US. After I returned to Vanderbilt, Dr. Cromwell stayed very supportive of me, inviting me to family dinners, Thanksgiving, and other holidays. After that, I would get many invitations to such dinners around the more elite community of Nashville. A local insurance executive and Vanderbilt alum once took me to an antebellum mansion on Franklin Road twelve miles south of town. He introduced me to authentic Southern gentile life, with all its beauty, furnishings, and refinement. His driveway was probably two city blocks, leading to an extraordinary house. The scene was beautiful at early sunset as the guests arrived. At the entrance of the house, there was a Confederate flag on the right side, and the American flag on the other. There was a grand entrance with chandeliers, uniformed black attendants on the outside, and butlers in tuxedos inside serving drinks and appetizers. There were no neighbors for a quarter mile in any direction.

The grueling third year of medical school was totally clinical and less academic. I was busy all day and night each day of the week. The internal medicine rotation was the most demanding part. I was given ten patients to follow intensively for three months. A typical day started with a 5 a.m. blood drawing, planned the previous night at about 10 p.m. with a group of internal medicine residents after we reviewed each patient on the floor. At 6 a.m., there were residents rounds in which each medical student gave brief presentations on his assigned patients and the latest issues along with proposed plans for the morning, after studying each case in the library and establishing priorities. When approved by the residents in charge, we were expected to carry out the plans. It was designed for us prospective doctors to test our physical and mental abilities and endurance to concentrate and carry out rational decisions under great stress. There were many near catastrophes and almost all of us had some sort of harrowing episode. Some students had to repeat this year in order to advance. One of the residents completely disappeared without a word. He was found somewhere in Florida ten days later and never returned to the program.

One morning at 5 a.m., having slept only three hours, I approached one of my seven patients to obtain brain spinal fluid through a lumbar puncture using a four-inch needle. It was my first lumbar puncture on a living body, though we had practiced a few times on each other in class. It is always scary to look at a four-inch needle, and even worse to insert it into someone's spine. The problem with the technique is the possibility of puncturing an artery, making it impossible to examine the cerebral-spinal fluid for the next few days, putting the patient at risk without credible test results. I woke up the patient for the test, introduced myself and the procedure. She responded positively, and then I asked, "Are you Mrs. Beckett?" She answered yes, so I nervously proceeded and got a clean tap of fluid without blood; but later that night, in front of professors and colleagues, it was discovered that I conducted the procedure on the wrong patient, since the lab results were inconsistent with the patient's condition. I realized that instead of asking her name, I should have checked her wristband with the name on my list. It was embarrassing; but the following day, I did another successful spinal tap.

In dire need of some reprieve from the grueling pace of school, I made plans to travel with a friend from New York the summer after third year. Sharon came to Nashville on a Greyhound; and we took my car through Mississippi, Louisiana, and Texas and down the Gulf coast of Mexico to Santa Cruz. The road led through increasingly dense vegetation in the rain forest, reminiscent of *Night of the Iguana*. As we traveled through the small jungle towns, we stopped for snacks and cerveza, witnessing the locals hunting iguana and roasting them over open flames on sticks for their evening meals. We stayed at cheap local inns, stopping at Indian markets in nearly every village. My Spanish from Compton College was enough to communicate the essentials; and I felt comfortable everywhere in Mexico, armed with antibiotics from school in case we got sick. We drove down toward Mexico City through increasingly dense forests without a clear destination. We decided to park the car and get a third-class train into the countryside toward Tapatula near the Guatemalan border. The train ride was three days and nights, slowly climbing hills into an ever-thickening jungle of amazing flora, waterfalls, and shaky bridges. At every train station, the locals sold fruit and pulque (fermented agave juice). By the time, we reached the Pacific coast in lower Mexico, we were eating a lot of boiled shrimp and grilled fish for just a few pesos—great for poor students like us. We enjoyed watching the interactions among the gregarious locals, children, goats, and chickens in the lively streets from the third-class train car.

We went to Guatemala and rode the local buses packed with peasants wearing their signature colors, indicating their tribal affiliations through the elaborate abstract patterns on their clothes. The various village members could identify each other through the clothing, as different clans had different colors and patterns. We often hitchhiked there, as it was easy to get rides; and the locals were eager to engage us and were kind and helpful. Occasionally we could hear them privately conversing about gringos and sensed their envy and perhaps hatred for the *Norte Americanos,* as they must have seemed over privileged and imperious at times, enjoying their vacations, expecting to be waited on, and other behavior born of arrogance or ignorance. We were so poor and young that I doubt they had those feelings for us, so we were not targets for theft or harassment.

By the beginning of the fourth year of medical school, I applied for a military internship with a commission in Boston. It was the height of the Vietnam War, and we all knew we would be drafted after our internships. I was commissioned as a Second Lieutenant in Boston in the following year. My rotation in psychiatry in the fourth year led me to work at the Central State Hospital by Dorothy Dix, a pioneer in mental health who convinced the federal and state governments to establish a mental hospital with more humanitarian principles and practices shortly after the Civil War.

Studying so many hours in close proximity with colleagues brought about significant relationships with my classmates. Tom from Atlanta and I moved into even two-bedroom apartment off campus with my fellow future psychiatrist, Tom, who was also in his second year. We shared a similar worldview, an extreme curiosity of our fellow man, including an incessant proclivity to English literature and philosophy.

Down the block from our place was a legendary spinster who lived alone, rarely venturing out of her unpainted, dilapidated house. She was rumored to have been left at the marriage altar decades ago which brought the onset of her prolonged reclusion. Her bedroom was upstairs, and its dimly lit window was the only sign of few ghostly shadow occasionally all the months we observed her. The light never went out in that room. We figured that sooner or later, she would have to come out; but she never did, and we never solved the mystery of the mysterious woman, though we heard many different versions of her background and tragedy over the years of rejection on wedding day; groom failed to show.

Tom and I found a nicer apartment the following year about a mile from the hospital, with two bedrooms, living room space for entertaining, and the kitchen. We would mix drinks and discuss T. S. Eliot's *The Wasteland, Four Quartets*, and *The Love Song* of Alfred Prufrock together, memorizing impressive phrases and debating various interpretations. We also read the groundbreaking philosopher-historian, Santayana, as well as new novels, like James Clavell's *King Rat* and Truman Capote's books. Another of our favorite exercises as budding psychiatrists was to clinically speculate on the personality of the literary characters such as T. S. Eliot!

Tom had many friends from Vanderbilt Undergradute School who were graduate students, and they often came to our place to visit and play. Several of them were passionate Romanticists and poets and continually chased girls at sorority parties. I sometimes tagged along the sororities at Vandy where were full of debutantes and the *crème de la crème* of Southern society.

One Saturday, at about 10 p.m., Tom and I were talking over a gin and tonic; and there was a knock on the door from an unannounced visitors. When we opened the door, we were shocked to see two gorgeous girls in beautiful Cambodian costumes carrying record albums under their arms, imploring us to let them come in to perform for us! We immediately thought they were undergrads from Vandy. I asked who they were; but they only smiled and coyly drew fans to their faces, staring back with smile. We lit candles as they requested; and they proceeded with an erotic dance, accompanied by traditional Cambodian music. We were then captives in our own house as they proceeded to show more and more exotic PLUMAGES. They smelled like apple. They mesmerized us! They then bid a sweet farewell with long kisses and disappeared into the darkness as we watched them walk away from our window, drop-jawed, and satiated. The next day, I asked Tom's friend, Simpson, what these two girls were all about, as he was known to be a rich playboy on campus. He pretended to know nothing about it, but grinned at me knowingly for the next several weeks. In retrospect, I can imagine concerned fraternity friends of Tom's seeing to it that we were entertained, as our stress level from the program was off the grid; and we must have seemed very anxious much of the time—and with so little time to date.

There was another semi mythological character in our group, a Vandy alum and close friend of Simpson, who lived as a groundskeeper and lived in the basement of a fashionable mansion owned by a single woman in Belle Meade, the classy neighborhood. He was about six-foot-two, so we called him "The Giant." During spring break, Tom, the Giant, and I drove to New Orleans and stayed with Simpson in his French Quarter apartment. When we visited the Giant's mansion, the lady of the manor, Betsy Howe, a stunning vibrant prima donna with piercing blue eyes and black hair combed straight back, came out to inspect the Giant's grounds work and to meet us. She knew we were medical students and spoke of her brother-in-law, a faculty member at our school, who happened to be one of our main professors in psychiatry. She was also related to several other influential people including dean of medical student (T. Billings) at Vanderbilt. The coincidence took us aback; and I realized what a small world this Southern gentility was, and how it operated with regard to establishing one's career. I knew I was in good with this group and truly enjoyed their company as well.

A month later, Betsy again sent us invitations for dinner where I socialized with my professors for the first time and met one of their friends, Thompson, who invented the Thompson submachine gun. Betsy was an infamous socialite known affectionately as the "Witch of Belle Meade," a genuine Nashville legend. Her clan had produced many intellectual and business virtuosos in Tennessee for generations. Her previous twelve-room mansion in Belmont where she lived alone burned to the ground under mysterious circumstances. She then moved into a current smaller stately mansion in Belle Meade where she lived also all alone. Rumor had it that she was a virgin—in fact, she herself had often alluded. Tom and I were curious about this well-educated gorgeous woman who seemed to enjoy playful young male Vanderbilt Medical School students. She again invited us for dinner weeks later, and I was surprised when she served only hot dogs on her formal dining table surrounded by heirloom décor. She drank quite a few gin and tonics that night and sent me for another bottle up in the attic as she told the stories behind the artifacts in her house to the rest of the group, including how her great grandfather was an assistant to Jefferson Davis.

During the summer, before our third year, Tom received a call from his mother's psychiatrist in Atlanta. He asked me to make the trip down with him to tend to her and consult with the doctor. We drove his Mustang convertible down and arrived on the stately knoll of their large two-story home on a ten-acre lot surrounded by old growth trees and a rushing stream. She was glad to see us, but clearly depressed, though she made a great effort to appear happy. She prepared dinner in the dining room and arranged with Tom to see her psychiatrist in the morning. The next day Tom's old high school friends came for a reunion down by the river where they used to gather. There were two young men and four young ladies. We all went waterskiing and had a barbeque with lots of beer down on the riverbank that hot and long summer's day.

After five years in military and specialty training in Psychiatry including Board Certification, I opened my private practice in Medical Arts Building within Vanderbilt Hospital ground in Nashville. My practice grew quickly and abundantly including consultation within The State of Tennessee Mental Health Department.

Chapter Twenty

Marriage

Darlene greeted me daily with a smile as I passed through the entrance of the hospital where she worked during the summer of 1965. For weeks, we had exchanged interested glances; and I asked her to have lunch with me in the cafeteria, which she happily accepted. She was a petite, proper, and very bright psychology major at nearby Belmont College, showing obvious interest in me as we discussed our hopes and dreams. Her father was the president of the Southern Baptist Convention with parishes in Nashville and its suburb, Franklin. We dated a few months; and I brought her back to my place and introduced her to Tom, who was supportive, but neutral. Although she was four years younger than me, she seemed mature for her age. We had many picnics and favorite hideaways in nature. I was not as serious about marriage as she was, as I planned to move to Boston in five months for internship. Her parents were puzzled over their errant daughter, as she was not interested in Christianity. Around this time, I finished my National Medical Graduate Exam, which enabled me to get a medical degree.

Because of our boiling intimacy, I had provided her with birth control pills through my clinic. Soon she got pregnant anyway and wanted to get married and go to Boston with me, creating a significant crisis in my life—the biggest dilemma I had ever had, as I did not plan on marrying her. I called Dr. Otto Billing, the famous psychoanalyst and one of my professors; but he said this was not a psychiatric problem, but a social issue. I did some more soul searching a month or so later, when Darlene confessed she had gotten pregnant on purpose to get me to marry her. I did not speak with her parents, but wrote to my dad in Korea. I asked her to abort, but she said she would carry the baby with or without me. A month before leaving for Boston, after much deliberation and introspection, I asked her father, Pastor Peters, to marry us in the chapel at Belmont College chapel.

Three months after the wedding of which my father informed, he sent me, a letter declaring that I was totally disinherited. He had apparently expected me to come back to Korea to support him and his family, though I never had considered leaving America. I would have happily brought him to Nashville though. This was the last exchange I had with my father, at least while he was alive. I often wonder if my marriage broke his heart, even though his health had already severely declined. In 1967, two months before medical school graduation, I received a telegram from Korea that my father had died.

Having received my order to begin internship in Boston on September 1, 1967, I bought my first new car, a Volkswagen Fastback, to make a trip to California to show Darlene the countryside and to thank the Putnams for supporting me through medical school and then drive back to Boston. We saw Aunt Merle and Uncle Ben in LA. Uncle Ben was still working construction and making his daily rounds, but had slowed down considerably. He no longer took out his prized blue Cadillac on Sundays, due to his infirmities. We then drove back across the desert and Rocky Mountain eastward to Boston though Darlene had to make frequent stops for nausea in her pregnancy. We made it back to Boston after a difficult trip, set up an apartment, and awaited the arrival of the baby.

The new internship was extremely busy. Each three-month rotation was internal medicine, ob/gyn, pediatrics, and surgery. I had to make an extensive presentation at the end of each rotation to the entire medical staff and some sixty doctors. It was in internal medicine where I met Father Allen Mulligan, who would be my son's godfather, good friend, and alter ego. I was taking care of a terminal case with multiple myeloma with metastasis, a form of lymphatic bone marrow cancer. While the man was clearly dying, I took care of him better than anybody expected, keeping him alive longer than the family believed possible. My ulterior motive was to see how long I could prolong his life. Finally one Tuesday evening at 10 p.m., I could see he was going to expire, so I called the attending priest to perform last rites of unction as required by his Catholic faith. Father Mulligan and the entire family came, waited, and prayed, while the unconscious patient dying. Waiting for him to pass turned out to be a marathon. During this time, Father Mulligan and I discussed many issues of life and death; and he taught me the Catholic worldview and Church notions of the hereafter. By 5 a.m., we were all exhausted; relatives had left and I had dozed off for a few hours. At 7 a.m., a nurse notified me that he had died peacefully with his sister watching over him.

The following January, I invited Father Mulligan to my home to baptize my newborn son, Alex, named after Alexander the Great, and asked him to be the godfather, as I didn't have any relatives nearby. We became lifelong friends, and later I was reassigned to Washington DC. I heard that Father Mulligan had also moved there. We were glad to meet up once again. I was surprised to learn he defrocked himself, leaving the Jesuit seminary in Boston to be a bachelor in Bethesda.

Meanwhile, Darlene, a true Southerner, yearned for her familiar Tennessee and was lost without it. Unlike me who relished new adventures in distant lands and was comfortable almost anywhere, she could not embrace new settings. She would go back to Nashville for extended periods, often with Alex. Allen and I ate dinner out or sampled his excellent French cooking, and there were many parties around town as we enjoyed our respective windows of freedom. We would joke about being a motley duo: a defrocked priest and an abandoned doctor, wandering the bars and restaurants of greater DC., talking philosophy, life and death, and the finer points of ethics and metaphysics. He eventually married a girl he dated during that time and they adopted two Korean children—a boy and a girl. I thought then about how great it would have been for me and Misa to have been adopted by such a couple from the onset. I am sure that I had something to do with his choice to adopt Korean orphans; and I began then to see how the great circle of life was operating through us, and how people are capable of touching each on a profound level across traditional fears and barriers for the benefit of all.

My second rotation of the internship was in the ob/gyn service at the Women's Lying Hospital where I delivered three or four babies a day for three months. Each episode was a long waiting period with several panicked minutes at the end prior to the arrival of a new baby. During the long waits through the night, I often watched TV with the other doctors, observing the escalation of the Vietnam War with Walter Cronkite. I trembled at the disturbing graphic images of bloody warfare and American casualties, remembering long suppressed similar images I saw as a child in Korea. Meanwhile the hippies were flocking to San Francisco, and families were divided over the war, making me recall the beatniks I'd talked to in Santa Rosa over ten years ago and the final speech of Eisenhower, warning of the "Military-industrial Complex." We could all feel the ripples of major social change before us.

The third rotation over the next three months in the pediatric emergency room contained my most traumatic experiences in Boston City Hospital. My additional duty involved monitoring fifteen sick and traumatized babies, some who had serious illnesses, and some who were unconscious. It was complicated to take care of sick babies that were so small and fragile—and troublesome to learn the causes of their trauma, as I felt helplessly unable to combat the neglect and abuse that continually brought them to the emergency room. There was a disturbing pattern of infants being tossed or fall from high-rise apartments, and I saw about twelve such cases during this time. The ambulances were bringing them in from the ghetto. I could not fathom how some of these babies often survived the fall with relatively little harm; but they were more often injured beyond belief, with no family members to claim them; and we often could not even identify them. It seemed like the world was going crazy; and Darlene and I were in trouble as well, and seemed to be losing the ability to communicate.

In mid-July of the following year, I received the order to report to a military hospital in Dallas. Darlene, Alex, and I drove down via Nashville, so Darlene's parents could see Alex. There were two high-security narcotic rehabilitation centers in the nation—one in Kentucky and the other in Fort Worth. They were run by the federal government for incarcerated narcotics offenders. When I arrived, there were 400 hard-core inmates housed underground with electric doors and long corridors. There were about twenty medical personnel and an equal number of support staff, social workers, and other professionals. It was a good place to practice medicine and psychotherapy, although I had not yet completed my formal residency. Once a week, all the staff members met in the conference room around a large round table with local professionals from all over the US and elsewhere to talk for two hours about rehabilitation theories and methods. This was the highlight of each week and very stimulating for me. We dealt with twenty patients each and implemented various specializations to rehabilitate the inmates. Steve Feinstein, my assistant and a dedicated, well-trained social worker from Boston was assigned with me to twenty inmates. We had broad authority for managing their physical and psychological rehabilitation. How to proceed to rehabilitate the older hard-core narcotics-addicted inmates was a difficult challenge, as our resources were limited. Once a month, there were consulting physicians soliciting our views and analyses on complicated issues.

The biggest problem I had was the mission to rehabilitate twenty patients in one year. Each day began with a two-hour group therapy session, assisted by a social worker. This was followed by individual daily visits with all twenty patients to go over the issues and potential options they had in rehabilitating toward discharge. Some of the discharges heavily influenced by our decisions and evaluations of their progress.

Brignac was from the French Quarter of New Orleans where he was a big-time narcotics dealer. We focused on him because we thought he was one of the few who could be rehabilitated. He was double-crossed by a business partner and a planted federal agent, captured and sentenced to federal prison. Toward the end of my year, he made significant progress; and I got to know him very well, spending more time with him than the other patients. I tested his progress by allowing him liberty outside the fence in preparation for discharge. His monitoring included unannounced blood and urine tests. We also monitored any contact from the outside and reviewed his relationships to make sure of his safety and readiness to reassimilate into society. I made a special request to the administration for his release on a two-week pass. Some patients were beyond rehabilitation, but Brignac had potential for complete recovery. In interviews with his wife from New Orleans, I prepared her for all the contingencies before I sent him home. Nine days after his release, I received notice that he had been shot to death by an old associate. I was naïve about these dangers and have often wondered if I may have rushed his rehabilitation as a result of my hopes for him. My love of labor lost.

Meanwhile I received a letter from Dr. Orr, my mentor and Chair of the Department of Psychiatry at Vanderbilt inviting me to the Vanderbilt residency program. He was saddened that I had already chosen to go to DC to join the National Institute of Mental Health. Dr. Orr too was related to "The Witch of Belle Meade" in Nashville and had many innovative ideas like rehinging his office door for patients to pull forward to open the door to give them more control over their lives—as opposed to pushing out into uncertainty. I admired and emulated his attention to detail and saw how it improved overall patient care, and there were imminent events that would test me severely, so I needed all the skills I could find.

Around this time, I took gliding training in Dallas, one of the highlights of my life, and flew solo for the first and last time. There was such a sublime silence and sense of time itself being suspended while I soared, riding the currents with a feeling of total freedom, almost as if I could touch God. I will never forget how radiant the sky looked as my heart raced, and I steered the glider along the curve of the planet looking over the great flat plane of Texas, so vast and barren below me.

Chapter Twenty-One

Julie Gives Us a Scare

In June 1968, I received orders to report to psychiatric residency at NIMH (National Institute of Mental Health) in Washington DC. We packed and sent our household ahead in boxes and drove from Dallas. Making this transition with a one-year-old was rough; but after much deliberation, we got a place on the east side of town, three blocks from the zoo in an ethnically diverse area—something that was always important to me. Because of my military service in Boston, I got good terms and had no pay no money down on the house. My neighbors on both sides were teachers. Every morning I drove through Rock Creek Park's curving roadway along the Potomac, past the Lincoln Memorial, Washington Monument, and the Watergate, and finally down river to Elizabeth Hospital where Abraham Lincoln's wife was confined due to her bipolar disorder. I visited the room that she lived in for decades. The Elizabeth Hospital excited me, as it continually had the most famous psychiatrists visiting from around the nation.

I was shocked that nine out of the twelve of residents were Jewish, with varying degrees of adherence to orthodox customs. I had no idea there were so many Jewish people in this country. There was also one black man, only one woman—and me. There was a strong clique among six of the Jewish residents—all from different parts of the northeast; while the other three were far more open to socializing with the rest of us. Steve Feinstein was married to a gentile and was strikingly intelligent, articulate, and inclusive of all his colleagues. I had many dinners at his house, and he would come to my place to listen to classical music and trade stories about our training. He was privately schooled all the way, and very privileged, yet had remarkable candor, soulfulness, and humility, unlike many of his peers.

I. DAVID HONG MD, US NAVY CAPTAIN, RETIRED

NIMH residency offered many opportunities with all its resources and national reputation. It sponsored trips for us to do psychodrama with the guru, Dr. Pearls, for a weekend seminar and dramatic playhouse enacting the psychological issues of each attendee. Many of the residents and trainees in the psychodrama workshop achieved a profound emotional catharsis as their past conflicts played out. This was a good time to enter psychoanalysis for the first year of my psychiatric residency to bring up any subconscious or unconscious issues. I was lucky to find an analyst within the federal agency system who agreed to take me once a week for one year. He was on government time, as I was also a government employee. We examined the possible unconscious motivations that drove me to inhabit the positions I found myself in since arriving in the US in 1956, such as my fundamentally unhappy marriage with Darlene. He also had me look into my dreams, one of which was being a frightened and determined pilot waiting for my mission in a fighter squadron during wartime, having been chosen to save the day with twenty other pilots.

I received a call around this time informing me that my old roommate, Tom, my soul mate for three years during the medical school days, had been found dead by the river a quarter mile downstream from his mother's house. To this day, I shudder at his unexplained death and remember him as my true brother and alter ego. Among all the losses in my life, this was perhaps the most painful. Of all the people I had met in America, I knew and loved Tom, my soul brother the most. That was just the beginning of the bad news that year.

In December of 1968, I received an emergency call from Nova Scotia from my sister, Julie, assisted by a local pastor from St. Johns. He asked me to come out immediately to help her. Julie had come to St. Johns to meet her fiancé, a Korean who was studying in Canada, and who I remembered seeing at my mother's office several times in Seoul, laden with copious gifts, which arrived continuously while I was in Korea. Julie's situation in Seoul had been hardly comfortable, living with my disabled father in poverty, having been rejected by my mother like all of us. For this reason, I had sent Julie a considerable amount of money that I managed to squeeze out of Mother. When she left Seoul, Julie was empty-handed with only the promise of my mother's wealth as an asset in her finding a husband. This man had courted her many years, bought many gifts, and was enraged that Mother offered no dowry. Julie was in a crisis with no place to go, so I purchased a round trip ticket to Nova Scotia. When I arrived in Boston to change planes, the airport was snowed in and no travel was possible for the foreseeable future. I stayed with a friend and made a call to INS explaining the problem and asked to speak to the officer in charge. When he called back, I told him of Julie's precarious condition due to physical and emotional trauma. I also suspected the man had beaten her. I asked how I could bring her to the US to stabilize her condition until I could sort things out for her. The agent decided she should get an immigration visa to come into the US under my supervision.

Julie came to live with me for about a month after taking my advice to visit Nami in Hollywood and Misa in Los Gatos. She had been calling me complaining of nightmares, sleeplessness, and disorientation, and wanted to come stay in my home. When she arrived, she was depressed and lamented her language limitations, which she feared, would impede her from ever getting ahead in this country. She found a menial job in DC at the Rock Creek Park Hilton Hotel. I was then separated from Darlene, who was spending a lot of time by herself in Nashville with Alex. Finally, Darlene came back from her mother's and asked me to accompany her to Nashville again, hoping to move back there with me. I was resistant, as DC was very stimulating for me, but agreed to a short visit.

This left Julie all alone in our house. When we returned after ten days in Nashville, there was much commotion in the neighborhood and an eerie atmosphere. As I approached the house, my neighbor rushed out to tell me that the ambulance had been there only one hour ago. He said that they had taken a young unconscious woman to the emergency room at DC hospital. The neighbor had called the police six hours ago, having heard a thump, because he did not think anyone was there after we had left. When the police entered, they found Julie lying on the stairs without any vital signs.

I dropped everything and raced down to meet the resident doctor who told me she needed to be moved to the morgue at any moment since there were still no vital signs, and there was facial and body necrosis due being motionless for days. I insisted he bring her out for me to see and found her in the exact condition he described. After some tears and insistence from me, he agreed to try a total body clysis infusing Ringer solution with multiple small needles in several parts of her body—slowly and with low pressure and warmer temperature. We surmised that she must have taken an overdose of pills, as I had a number of assorted samples throughout the house. Miraculously, twenty-four hours later, there was a faint heartbeat on the EKG. On the following day, she had twitching movements, though still totally unconscious.

She remained unconscious for fourteen days, with increasing spastic movements and eventually some moaning. By the third week, she was able to recognize me, but could not remember what had happened to her. She had severe necrosis of her cheekbone down to bare bone on one cheek and the same on other parts of her body. Her kidneys were severely damaged with low blood flow, and this had ominous implications for her future. She was fully conscious and talking after a month, I then consulted the NIMH supervising suicidologist about how I could help rehabilitate her.

The more she became aware of her situation, the more she cried. She could not express anything but profuse tears and overwhelming grief. I let her cry to her heart's content, knowing that this was part of her recovery, but desperately wanted to know what she was crying about. She went through a gauntlet of physical and emotional suffering beyond my comprehension. I was most concerned with permanent brain damage. For the next several years, she lived in deep depression and her cheekbone, unable to fully heal, remained covered with gauze. Her recovery was extremely slow, and she went through multiple plastic surgeries to close the wound. Her expenses were over $25,000, which I could not afford. Since she was a landed immigrant, I helped her apply for welfare, which paid her medical bills.

A few years later, she became a born-again Christian and found a renewed appetite for life. She tried to get a job, and got around via city buses with some assistance. Gradually she became autonomous and never complained about her difficulties again. She continued at the nearby Hilton Hotel, and later was promoted to food and beverage buyer. She regained her intellectual capacity and worked there for several years, eventually becoming a CPA, and was later promoted to chief purchaser by her fourth year. In spite of the scars on her face, she had better judgment and a better personality than before, and eventually met a young coworker at the hotel—a self-defrocked Catholic priest named Russell. They were kindred spirits and ventured into a new world together. Russell went on to get a PhD and became a federal consultant while she got into real estate license and financial advising. They bought a house together on a one-acre lot on the Potomac outside of DC and had successful three sons. Having retired for sometime, she has been spending most of her time in civic volunteer projects in metropolitan DC.

Chapter Twenty-Two

Life on the Farm

Early in 1971, I decided I wanted to practice psychiatry in DC and had already had received referrals from the Korean embassy. However, I reluctantly agreed to go back to Nashville since Darlene insisted she would never be happy in DC. She was also less than excited in Boston and Texas, always yearning to return to Nashville. I could be happy almost anywhere; so after consulting with friends, I agreed to try Nashville one more time and applied for my final year of residency at Vanderbilt. We bought a modest home south of Hillsboro Road, but Darlene was still unhappy and decided she wanted a divorce without any reason. I gave it to her, along with all my cash, but kept the house. I was shaken and restless, as if the ground had broken beneath me, and I needed to find terra firma again, away from the bad memories and trauma of our painful separation.

At the same time, my office secretary was moving out of town, another smaller crisis. I asked my ex-mother-in-law, Florine, to find me a secretary, as she had many contacts through her church in Franklin, fifteen miles south of my office. She surprisingly called me back within days and asked, "How about *me* working for you?" She immediately started efficiently organizing my office, for which I thanked her, as always. She also found me a good house cleaner who cooked, and my life was restored some equilibrium. The housekeeper came at 8 a.m. every Monday, cleaned and made a five-pound roast in the oven at 6:30 p.m. with table settings for two to keep me going for the week. I barely ever saw her, and avoided her as well, as she was quite attractive. Thus, my life was regulated with the essentials so I could focus on the hard work of establishing a practice. Sometimes I worked sixteen hours a day, plus weekends over the next year and a half. In retrospect I think Florine helped me in acknowledgement that I got

I. DAVID HONG MD, US NAVY CAPTAIN, RETIRED

somewhat raked in the divorce, and understanding that my well-being and that of my practice was best for her grandchild, and ultimately her daughter as well. Maybe she also hoped that Darlene and I would reconcile.

I decided I would like to become a part-time farmer and rancher, raising Angus cattle and riding horses somewhere in the rolling hills of Columbia, Tennessee. I dreamed of owning a house and a large barn that held 1000 bales of hay to raise a few dozen cows during the winter. I loved the wooded hills and flat fields and fertile land and wanted over a hundred acres with a creek and a pond. I needed such a peaceful retreat and communion with nature where I could work out my frustrations and be with the animals, similar to how I did at the orphanage.

To pull this off, I needed help from one of my colleagues, Dr. Fulton Greer, who lived in Franklin, and whose father was a judge in town. He had asked me to consult a number of times in his office; and eventually I practiced a day a week there, instead of having patients drive twenty-five miles to my office. I also had consulted Dr. Greer as he had to keep a revolver in his office because one of his patients was seriously threatening him. He had no place to go in the small town because everyone knew his routine. I contacted his angry patient to have him vent his grievances and the turmoil subsided. I asked him to help me look for a piece of land because he grew up in the area that I was interested in and also owned a several-hundred acre farm nearby. His partner, another doctor, owned the adjoining 600-acre farm with a big pond and agreed to help me find a place. One day we got in his Cadillac and drove from his office to his 600-acre spread. Somewhere out of town, he pulled over and dropped a line from the car to fish a while with the engine still running. I was pleasantly amazed at how in a matter of minutes he caught a foot-long trout. I knew that this way of life was exactly what I wanted.

One day I drove through the hills until I reached a mile-long driveway through his property at the top of which was a fierce, growling German Shepherd running loose, a sign I should have heeded from the onset. I could not get out of the car, so he came out and held the dog down so I could go inside and discuss the land possibilities. He told me he found a 130-acre farm adjoining his property that he wanted to show me. It was covered with mature oaks and bordered his property so I could walk down and fish on his creek anytime I wanted. I walked all over the land; and I decided to buy it from the owner, Connie Andrews.

I imagined a thousand pounds of tobacco hung to dry in the barn to sell in the spring. There were also eighty head of Black Angus. Connie was completely self-sufficient and grew the government allotted amount of tobacco on four acres of plowable land. He also had thousands of bales of hay already stacked three stories high in the barn. He worked the land with his wife and had been raised in that same house. It was as if my imagination of what I desired had produced this property to exact specifications for me. My wish had been fulfilled—and quickly.

I also met his sharecropper, a mulatto man named McGee who lived alone in "the hollows" about a mile down the road on ten acres on the hillside and worked with a mule that he raised himself. He had a car, electricity, a fireplace, and a cluttered yard, and had also had been born nearby. His income was strictly from tobacco sales and livestock. I was curious how a black man lived in the white part of town and was happy to see him content and successful, and later hired him as my sharecropper to raise tobacco. I played with Alex, who was then six and already in love with the farm, frolicking around on bales of straw under the tobacco sticks that hung from the ceiling.

Dr. Greer suggested what this land was worth, and I paid it at $80,000. I bought a horse and put a hitch on my Chevy Nova to pull the trailer. I also got a pony for Alex so that we could ride together through the hills and pastures. It was very demanding to keep up with the animals' needs, the pastures, and the fences. As the months passed, our enthusiasm for the farm waned due to all the work. My horse, Caesar, became estranged to the extent that he would not come to me, because he often would not see me for weeks at a time. I had to bribe him with sweet oats, but even so, he came down less and less, and became somewhat wild when I tried to mount him. I could not inspect my cattle on the hills and was called once by the neighbors, saying that one of my cows had delivered a calf at midnight with considerable distress. It was nearly impossible for me to tend to it from twenty-five miles away. I realized that cows needed midwives just like women, especially in breach birth. One time I went out to the pasture to find a distraught calf running around a dead cow.

I had purchased a Fiat convertible and one day took Alex to the farm to ride together. It took a few hours of climbing the hills, trying to entice Caesar so I could saddle him. I finally succeeded, and Alex rode his pony while I rode the semi wild stallion. He suddenly galloped and abruptly put his head down; and I tumbled over the top of him and landed on my hand, nearly breaking it. It was so bruised that I could not handle the gearshift on the Fiat. I quickly taught Alex how to shift through the gears while I worked the clutch with my foot. He was very proud, as he shifted the gears all the way home, before I had to go the emergency room.

Chapter Twenty-Three

Trouble on the Farm and "The Man in Black"

Connie was very helpful, giving me good advice about harvesting lumber on my property and how to sell it for a reasonable price. He was a church-going man but barely knew how to read and write, though he was quite smart. He was a hard worker, did not drink, and always went to church every Sunday. He often entertained me with dinners at his house; and I would stop by and ask for practical advice, including how to work the farm. He finally confided in me one day that Dr. Fulton had come around a month after I purchased the land to ask for a finder's fee, but Connie had never agreed to this. He thought it was improper, but gave him the money anyway, because as he said, "I got a good price from Mr. Hong." Connie confessed to me that I had been overcharged.

I was having difficulties managing the large property and all the livestock, so I put the land up for sale. I felt betrayed by Fulton Greer, and Connie agreed that I had been wronged. I could not forget about it for the next few years, and an attorney I asked agreed that it was illegal to receive a finder's fee without real estate license. Without knowing how the system worked, I started a lawsuit to learn how the American legal system worked. My main motive was to see the core value of the white Americans in the rural South. Since Greer's father had been the chief county judge for years, I hesitated. On the other hand, I did not see any influence in Greer's favor since his father would not be involved in hearing the case, which to my surprise I eventually won through jury trial which I asked through which I was impressed of jury members imbued with Christian values and once again, the American justice system helped me and served the spirit of the law with justice. As an Asian and an outsider making a case against a local "good ole boy" I had doubts initially as to how fair the outcome would be, but had to test it. My faith in American system was reconfirmed.

Around this time, I was assisting a physician at the Vanderbilt University Hospital who had just received a memorable admission, the music legend Johnny Cash, "The Man in Black." He had been battling substance abuse for some time, had finally reached a critical condition, and was in a state of exhaustion with damage. I was charged with checking on him with another psychiatrist. Once I entered his room on my daily rounds to check his vital signs and then I asked him how he was doing, he had a distant look in his eyes, as if he were gazing out somewhere far beyond the hospital room. He said that he had accepted his savior and was ready for God's Kingdom. I told him that he might have to wait a while longer because our whole staff was committed to helping him rehabilitate. Then he asked me, "Do you believe in heaven and hell, Dr. Hong?" I told him that I was just a doctor and not a true theologian and suggested that what I thought did not matter, but that I was a Christian and believed in salvation. He perked up a bit, even smiled faintly and said, "Good, that's good."

Sometimes I would hear him humming as I passed and wondered if he was composing beautiful songs that might be recorded later. I smiled to think that a doctor can actually help bring more music into the world. Before Cash left, he reached out to grab my hand and thanked me with solemn sincerity and said, "I guess heaven can wait a little while." I was happy to hear later that he stayed drug free and sober for a long time after that and that his recording career blossomed again.

My practice in Nashville continued to grow. As a consultant to an outlying community thirty miles away, I met an energetic health worker and a good psychologist, Wyatt Harper, who had recently returned to the US after years in the mountains of Vietnam as a communications officer. He had listened to all the traffic from both sides of the front to determine what the Russians and Chinese were doing to supply the North Vietnamese. He came from a solid family and went to Amherst College, but his parents were distant with him. He came to live in Tennessee after he was discharged from the service in Kentucky. He was lonely, intellectual, and articulate, and proposed that we start a private practice together. I went once a week to Dixon to consult his patients and prescribe medications. I also provided all the equipment and office furnishings. I leased an office at a hospital there, put our shingle on the door, and asked for referrals, which came abundantly. He did good work, and I enjoyed driving on I-40 into Dixon forty miles west of Nashville once a week. I saw the most serious cases and transferred them to the hospital in Nashville where I usually had several inpatients at any given time. For years, we worked well together; but he needed closer support, and was usually in conflict with his woman at any given time, and adjustments to the new practice were difficult for him. He also needed to be in a bigger town. I consulted him in my home, having him stay overnight and weekends for a few years. This was the first time that I felt I was able to be a true mentor to someone, and I became quite invested in his success and would keep track of him for many years after and even to days. When I left Nashville, he shed tears as I departed on my new venture, as if I were leaving a dear little brother behind—but my work was taking me elsewhere; and I had more service to offer my country, something he understood quite well as a veteran.

Chapter Twenty-four

Kim Arrives: The Love of My Life

In 1973, when I returned to Father's empty home for a visit, I retrieved his remains from the Buddhist temple where they had been stored for several years. I walked with the urn around the beautiful temple gardens, listening to the tricking of fountains and taking in the beauty of the grounds and lotus blossoms floating on the pond—all the things father loved. I walked him up to a gazebo under a wisteria tree, just like the one that he spent countless hours in, puffing his American tobacco, visiting friends, and looking over his beloved garden. I could feel not only the presence of his spirit, but a common spirit that we inhabited together. I prayed and then dipped my wet finger into the urn and held it to my tongue in remembrance and complete acceptance of who he was. As I tasted his mortal remains, a flood of memory washed over me along with a tremendous feeling of compassion and love for him. When I tasted his ashes, I remembered the smell of his briarwood pipe and Japanese cologne. I remembered his arms sheltering me, and me walking in the shadow of his huge frame along the roads and rivers of Korea amid mortar fire and soldiers. I have no idea how appropriate it was to ingest him. I have since read that some aboriginal cultures in South America do this. I also came into a feeling of radical acceptance of myself along with forgiveness of any transgressions I may have committed within my family. I knew then, as I always really knew, that Father and I were joined forever as companions in survival—best friends, as well as father and son. And strangely enough, after I performed this self-designed ritual, the one thing that had separated us in the later years of his life was remedied, as I once again had my feet on native soil, and destiny would work its way. Later, my half brother disposed of the rest of Father's remains into the Han River.

I. DAVID HONG MD, US NAVY CAPTAIN, RETIRED

After an impulsive failed marriage to former model turned cardiac care nurse at Vanderbilt hospital, I was disillusioned with the whole realm of love and marriage, then after much thought decided to find a good Korean woman, just as Dad had so relentlessly urged. Since I was a well-established doctor in my early thirties, many calls came offering to set me up on dates; but I had been exchanging letters for a year with a nurse named Kim from the National Medical Center and decided to go to Korea to meet her. After a week of dating, she suggested we visit a newly created national folk village twenty miles south of Seoul that depicted the ancient ways of Korean life.

We took a bus and many taxis and arrived after two hours of traveling over dusty, hot roads in what was beginning to feel like a sacred pilgrimage to the core of my heritage with my own personal angel. I was looking for a Kleenex but could not find one, and Kim took out her handkerchief and gave it to me. It was embroidered and neatly folded twice. When I unfolded it to blow my nose, I was surprised by the sweet fragrance, just as I had been intoxicated by Charlotte's perfume years ago, but in this case, it was as if Kim were sent specifically for me, like an answer to a prayer. Her cleanliness, grace, and ingenuity made me overwhelmingly attracted to her. She seemed to defy a world that was getting increasingly crude. Maybe it was an auspicious alignment of the stars or a strange confluence of our paths that joined in a moment of magic; but I asked her to marry me right there—and to this day she is just as beautiful and graceful as at that magical moment.

We married in the spring of 1975, and the next few years were quite difficult for her as she tried to assimilate into American culture and language. I tried to teach her how to drive, which was awkward at best. Eventually she earned a license, but rolled our Volvo driving down a dirt road to our farm in Nashville—miraculously escaping without a scratch. I was very busy in my office, and she needed a woman to introduce her into social circles. My secretary, Delores, had a sweet Southern Baptist spirit and initiated Kim's Americanization. I asked her to do extra duties on paid time, like taking Kim around Nashville, shopping, and exploring the communities from the lowest level first. Delores taught Kim the song, "Jesus Loves Me, This I Know" in order to begin Americanization. They sang it over and over on a trip to Memphis—so I heard. Delores and her husband became our good friends over the years including plans to stay at their home for a few days for the 40th reunion of Vanderbilt medical school, class' 1967

As soon as I married Kim, she insisted that we get a new home where nobody had lived before because she believed there were ghosts in the old house. I like ghosts and spirits which are our own internal projections, however I concede to make her more comfortable. Delores recommended a property in a newly developed area, and we hired a realtor who helped us find a beautiful new home on a half-acre wooded lot on a circular drive. Kim was giddy about the new place and began happily decorating and furnishing it. Across our large backyard lived another couple with a son Alex's age. We had many cookouts at each other's houses; and the two boys became good friends, riding their bicycles through the yards. Sometimes we went hunting on my farm.

Gary was an affable businessman from Minnesota who came to the South to manage a computer technology-related business. Two couples in each convertible sport car raced down to Florida for a vacation and rented a small fishing boat off the beach of Panama City. We caught fish and crabs by the dozens on the bayou and cooked them outside our hotel. While we spread out some newspapers, shelled and ate the crabs with cold beer, we noticed a large condominium across the street with 70 two-story units on a beautiful lot with all the amenities including direct access to white sand beach. We saw that they had been auctioned the previous night and that the prices were reasonable, so we put some money down in case any of the buyers backed out or could not pay. A few weeks later, we got the condos; and for the next four years went down twice year, living in luxury and sailing, catching crabs, fish, and shrimp. Our kids loved it and many of our relatives and friends stayed at those condos, which we kept for many years until we moved to Seattle.

It occurred to me one night as Gary and I were smoking one of his Nicaraguan cigars on my terrace after a sunset crabbing excursion (how would Father have loved the taste of that cigar!) that by all assessments, I had truly experienced the heart of the American Dream. I wandered off a boat in San Francisco in 1956 with two antique vases and $100 sewn into my jacket lining with a truly tenuous future, and was now in near bliss in my own vacation home in what seemed like paradise. What had I done to deserve all this?

Chapter Twenty-Five

Dangerous Duty in Korea

Kim told me much of the Korea that I had forgotten. My curiosity gradually increased; and I decided to reexperience the old world with a new perspective, having lived a most un-Korean life for a quarter century. I decided to reenter the service and sent a letter to the Pentagon with my CV, specifically asking to be assigned to the Seoul area with the US Army. Three weeks later, I received a letter with an interview date and an airplane ticket with accommodations in the Pentagon where I met Col. Turner who was about to be assigned as the commander of the old MASH Hospital, now known as the 121 Evacuation Hospital. Thus, within three years of marrying Kim, I took my bride to Seoul where I found her. We sold our Brentwood house and half of the farm. I would return to Seoul as one of the American soldiers I idolized as a boy.

Shortly thereafter, I received orders to proceed to San Antonio for one month of oversea deployment training with my family. I closed my office and shipped our belongings ahead. Kim, our new daughter Lisa, and Alex handled it all well; and Kim was expecting our second child. The one-month training in San Antonio was much more than I had received previously, since I was going to a potential battleground. After the training, we drove the old Chrysler to Seattle to ship it to Korea. I was so impressed with the lush green land, crisp air, snow-capped mountain peaks, and shining lakes, that I decided we would come back there and buy a home.

The 121 Evac Hospital was at the center of Seoul near the South Gate of the old kingdom where all the foreign occupying forces have stayed over the centuries. It was just north of the old Han River railroad bridge. Two months after me, Kim arrived with Alex and Lisa. We had a very comfortable house with air-conditioning, reliable electricity, and heating which was difficult to obtain on the outside market.

WITH ONLY THE BEAT OF MY HEART

As expected, my duty at the 121 Evac Hospital was half time taking care of patients on the psychiatric ward, and half time in the afternoon in the outpatient clinic. There was an unending supply of patients; and all the doctors, regardless of their specialty, were in rotation for the emergency room.

The most traumatic experience I had in the two years of duty at this hospital began with a seemingly routine call on a slow Saturday. I received a panicked call from a medic in a helicopter that he was sending five severely wounded soldiers from the DMZ in twenty minutes. Assessment of the injuries required several doctors in all specialties, particularly orthopedic. Within seconds, I alerted the on-call surgeons and other staff who arrived immediately. In fifteen minutes, I heard the roar of the helicopter, followed by a stream of several stretchers with IVs running into barely conscious soldiers to stave of the massive blood loss. There was no time to lose, and I waved them into the waiting surgeons in the OR. Everything apparently went well, since I did not hear of casualties, but I was bothered that I had no means to follow up on their progress, which still bothers me today. When I asked up the chain of command, my superior would not disclose any details except you did your duty well.

At the beginning of the second year of my tour, I received a call from the chief of psychiatry that Col. Turner, the hospital commander, was alarmed at having lost two soldiers to suicide within a period of a few months. Little explanation was given as to the nature of the problem, but I understood we had to do something. My job was to evaluate, consult with command and treat soldiers, and set a course of action. I was amazed that I was being asked to do this, but it was an order that could not be refused. I feared for my life to be sent to the DMZ.

Arrangements were made every Monday morning for a military sedan to pick me up at the hospital at 7:30 a.m. to transport me to top-secret locations. Only the *Katsua*, Korean soldiers attached to the American forces, knew exactly where to go. I was the lone passenger in the backseat of the car that was marked "Command 121 Evac Hospital." The driver took me through familiar highways, which gradually branched into smaller and smaller bumpy dirt roads, passing many MP checkpoints along the way. The MPs saluted as we passed still more gates toward the final destination to see the patients and consult with the commanding officers. I arranged follow-ups until there was satisfactory resolution to the problems. Some of the patients were evacuated to our hospital on my recommendation until they recovered, and then were returned to active duty in the DMZ. Over a span of about six months, I became more comfortable with the DMZ and would ask the driver to take detours and different routes back to the hospital so I could observe the remote military installations. I also imposed myself on the command of a nearby Korean tank battalion to experience their mode of operation and was afterwards invited for tea with the officers. They seemed to enjoy the break from their isolated routine. Eventually the epidemic of anxiety in the DMZ subsided, and I was sent back to my regular duties at the Evac Hospital. From that point on, I occasionally received similar requests from high command, and once accompanied the Colonel and other officers to inspect another medical branch near Kunsan AFB, three hours south of Seoul.

Another time I was asked by the Colonel to accompany him and his sergeant via helicopter to Chun-Chon on a remote outpost in the eastern mountains near the DMZ to inspect and consult on the northeast front. This was the first time I ever flew in a helicopter in Korea. I wore a headset in order to listen to the air traffic and consult with my commander while flying above the mountains. The trip took only an hour and a half by air instead of the several hours it would take on the mountainous roads. I was impressed by the efficiency and cooperation displayed between the commander and the sergeant major. I was truly proud to be wearing the uniform of the US Army, knowing that our mission was vital and conducted with integrity in order to secure freedom and safety for my own people, and as an *American*. My life was truly making sense to me now to be protecting and empowering the people that had suffered with me all those years ago—something I might never have been able to do as a Korean citizen.

By this time, my department chief, Lt. Col. Wamble, was irritated and almost jealous, I think since his allocation of work increased among the remaining psychiatrists when I was on special missions like this. Yet another order came through our chief that the Col. Commander wanted me to accompany him to a hospital to see the family of a Korean civilian in who was injured by an Army truck. It was a goodwill gesture on our part to deliver a bundle of Korean cash to the mother of the young man while I translated the army's apology and willingness to pay the hospital costs. The family was deeply moved.

Soon I was up for my annual leave for a two-week vacation. Kim and I went to Thailand, since we now had a live-in maid to take care of the three kids, including our newborn son, Robert. We also visited Singapore and were impressed with its cleanliness and civic order. Soon I was called back again to participate in the chief's weekly staff meetings where a considerable controversy was brewing as to whether or not the hospital could afford to take on another project when there were insufficient funds and manpower for existing projects and regular hospital operations. The commander's position was that the hospital needed a special alcohol treatment center since so many soldiers were drinking excessively and having a variety of related health and behavior problems, such as traffic accidents related to alcohol, many of which were bad PR in the civilian communities. The deputy commander, the chief of professional services, was against the center. The commander finally decided in favor of the facility, and I was put in charge of ordering all the equipment and furniture and asked to start as soon as personnel were trained and assigned. Once the decision was made and the orders followed, there was no controversy; and the entire hospital cooperated.

I was totally removed from my colleagues and given an eight-person staff, and we were then told to train and organize ourselves to receive patients as soon as the furniture arrived. I designed the floor layout for various operations so as to accommodate up to a dozen patients at once. Meanwhile the commander asked me to go to San Diego Naval Command to receive training that is more special. I also attended an American Psychiatric Association meeting to further my alcohol-related medical expertise. I returned to Korea a month later and the furniture had arrived, and I assigned my staff their positions to start accepting patients for alcohol rehabilitation. Some of the lower-ranking officers were difficult; but the supervisor, Sergeant Hoagies, who disciplined them through me, was extremely receptive and cooperative. Before long, the program was successful; and I was discharged on schedule six months later. During my last days of duty at the hospital, I attended the promotion ceremony of Colonel Turner as he had become a general. The last time I was in Seoul, some fifteen years ago, the alcohol treatment program was still in operation. In 2005 I met General Turner in Bellevue, WA. I invited him to my home reflecting together all the events in DMZ and the creation of new ATF alcohol treatment facility at the Mash Hospital.

While on leave, I went pheasant hunting on Cheju Island, between Japan and Korea. We flew down and were picked up by army personnel and assigned lodgings. The next morning began with the sound of yelping hunting dogs eager to accompany us and our local guide. We were led to an abandoned Japanese WWII fighter plane base. All the cement bunkers and runways were in tact, though overgrown with trees and bushes sprouting through the cracks in the cement—a haven for hiding pheasants! I met some GIs who were riding motorcycles on the hillside trails having fun. When I returned to the Evac Hospital, I ordered a Suzuki RM 80 cc for Alex then eleven years old, along with a silver outer space like protective garment and helmet. He actually frightened the farmers in the remote villages in the mountains suddenly appearing with a roar from behind embankments and foliage like a space alien. We rode in tandem, me on a Honda XR Enduro 190, and went out as far as twenty miles from Seoul, sometimes into unknown villages that were inaccessible to trucks.

Chapter Twenty-Six

I Am David

My given name, Inpow, is difficult for people to remember, easily misspelled and always mispronounced. Even worse were the constant apologies from people for screwing up my name in various ways. I decided to give myself a new name that would be easy for others to remember, and my application for another military commission gave me the opportunity. I gave myself the middle name of David and began using it as my first name. There are no middle names in Korea, but only three syllables. To this day, my Korean patients' names in my office are confusing for my secretary who often misfiles them by using the last syllable as a last name. I have misplaced a lot of charts due to this!

I chose the biblical name of David, of whom there are so many hair-raising and compelling stories, largely because he consolidated the fractured tribes of Israel and dealt with human frailty. I have often thought of my own ancestry in terms of a fractured tribe, not only due to the war, but family strife as well. By taking an American name, I affirmed my true identity as an American, just as I had when I applied for citizenship and had to make my case as a conscientious objector. There is power in names and virtue in titling ourselves according to our nature, as our identities are constantly evolving. Year 2007, my wife and I visited Israel remembering how I changed the name to David, and thinking the related sacred geography and rich history of that holy land differently than I would have had I not acknowledged that part of me—a true world citizen. As I approach my later years, I can see how I was destined to play a part in unifying people of disparate origins through my work and travels. Where once I was concerned primarily with personal accomplishments and surmounting great challenges to test my abilities, even though I was often directly helping people through my practice, now my life is much more about affirming our shared humanity through my interactions with others. I truly believe that we are all ambassadors to one great world nation, and we each find our means of contribution if we heartily assume that responsibility. Thus I carry a Korean-American name and cross many national boundaries as a Christian, as a physician, as a former officer in the military, as a father, husband, and perpetual student of the human condition. I firmly believe we have a great deal to lose through unnecessary fear of others and their customs, and therefore have a *responsibility* to cross into uncertain arenas at times for the sake of greater harmony and understanding in a world that has the capacity to become increasingly ignorant and brutal. Therefore, I do not exchange one name for another, rather keep them both, keep them all—and who knows, there may be more yet to come.

Chapter Twenty-Seven

Washington State and Another Tour of Duty

In June of 1980, I was discharged from the army to the reserves, and we boarded a plane from Osan AFB to Seattle where we had already decided to resettle. We rented a house on Mercer Island for three months as we looked for our own place, as well as an office set up for me. Alex, now twelve, went back to Nashville with his mother as Darlene and I had agreed. I could not convince her to postpone receiving him, which I thought was best, since she was working full time; and we could provide more stability. There was often no one at home to watch him after school—a warning sign; but I hoped Darlene's mom would watch over him as well. At that time in Seattle, all kids were bused up to twenty miles from home starting at first grade, which bothered me. To avoid this, we settled in the small town of Medina by a small meandering creek filled with crayfish, minnows, and every spring, a pair of mating ducks. At the same time, I applied for a University of Washington psychiatry faculty position and received an associate clinical professorship where I worked two days a week for two years. I also found a group of four doctors, called the Harvard Psychiatric Group, in downtown Seattle, where I subleased one of the offices and started another practice, which rapidly took off. One year later, I made a big move to design my own suite in the Cabrini Tower in downtown Seattle. I took suite 707—symbolic of my love of flight and worked there for the next twenty-two years until I retired.

At home, my daughter had interacted mostly with our live-in housekeeper and Kim in Korea for two years, and therefore spoke very little English. We put her in kindergarten at St. Thomas Episcopal Church three blocks away; and when I visited her at school, I saw her playing all by herself, since she could not communicate with the other kids. Thereafter, I told Kim I would only speak English to the kids.

The adventures of parenting were only beginning. When Lisa was learning to walk, Kim and I told her to stay in the safe area that we had showed her. She immediately tried to escape the imposed boundaries and fell, bumping her head on the edge of a table and tearing it open. We took her to a park once, when she was around six, and she got on the swing and fearlessly begged me to push her higher and higher. She craved any activity that sent her soaring in the air or moving at high speeds—a true Hong! She skied vigorously and became the organizer of the university ski club and went on a deep Canadian excursion where she sustained knee and shoulder injuries, which required surgeries. Lisa continued in elementary education at Lakeside School after rigorous screening and interviews and eventually entered the University of Washington. After graduating, she traveled to Asia for six months. When she came home, she found a job and worked for another six months, then decided she must see Europe. When she returned, she entered the University of Washington and received her doctorate in audiology. While Lisa possessed true Hong wanderlust, I wanted to give her what my mother's side of the family had almost systematically tried to deny me and my younger sisters—absolute support for her education and the chance to pursue her dreams.

Bobby kept the family tradition by going to Lakeside and then went to the business school at Babson College in Wellesley, Massachusetts. After graduation, he taught in Korea for a year and stayed in Southeast Asia traveling between Korea and the Philippines working in international business involving oil importing.

Kim and I took the kids to the mountains one hundred miles northeast of our home during spring break one year, and we came upon a glacial stream with a big suspension bridge above the rushing water. Woven, cross-wooded panels were supported by two lone steel ropes across the stream. It was wobbly and downright scary to cross, with a flimsy-looking rope guard on both sides. I decided to venture out on the bridge, intending to go near the middle and then turn back. I asked the kids if they wanted to come with me. Both of them wanted to do it by themselves by holding tightly to the rope. I felt they could do it and wanted to see how well they could tolerate the risk. Lisa went first, following confidently behind me and, of course, wanted to go all the way to the other side, which I would not allow. Bobby stopped after a dozen steps, when he saw the rushing water below saying that he did not want to go any further and patiently waited for us to proceed back. A dozen or so steps further, I yelled, "Daddy needs help! Can you come help me?" I was surprised when he replied, "I'll help you when I grow up, Daddy, but not now." I was delighted.

Having successfully established my practice in Seattle, I turned to finishing my career in the military as a psychiatrist in the Medical Corps, which took a full weekend each month, plus two weeks of active duty per year for over twenty-two years. The trip from Bellevue to Fort Lewis was an hour each way, but the Naval Reserve at Sand

I. DAVID HONG MD, US NAVY CAPTAIN, RETIRED

Point was only five miles from our house; so I resigned from the Army and asked for a commission in the US Navy at Sand Point. It was a demanding commitment for the next sixteen years, since I already had been full-time active duty for six years.

I received a call for active duty aboard the Nimitz aircraft carrier to participate in a Western Pacific war exercise involving the Japanese, Australian, and Canadian navies. I took the family on a leisurely trip along the Pacific Coast Highway to San Diego, where I boarded the Nimitz. Kim drove back with the kids at the end while I boarded and assumed full-time duty seeing service men, including officers who were often falling into suicidal depression after leaving wives, girlfriends, and family behind without any means of communicating with them. Stateside mail arrived on deck once a week. I was alarmed at the number of other conflicts, interpersonal relationship problems, and other complaints among the personnel on deck. The possibility of undesired extended deployment was stressful for the sailors. I was the only Psychiatrist on board to serve 3000 personnel, seeing seven cases a day, and luckily no suicides.

As a Navy Captain, I was able to roam around as I pleased, including the bomb storage area at the center of the ship. It was accessible only through a heavy-duty elevator, which was separately controlled by its own power source. There I received a demonstration of how to assemble various bombs, from 200 to 2000 pounds with different fuses attached at the noses depending on whether they were for land targets, or incendiary bombs for large areas. During the exercise, there was a simulated enemy attack with four days and nights of continuous landing and taking off. I watched a defending missile obliterate an incoming missile at extremely high speed. I was surprised at the lack of pyrotechnics, as it was a nearly invisible puff of smoke, gone almost as soon as it happened.

I also consulted in the Navy brig, maintaining the mental and physical health of the prisoners while they served their decreed punishments. I was surprised that they were given only bread and water, according to the rules of the old colonial days. While I was somewhat impressed by their unusual procedures, I took it upon myself to provide vitamin supplements somewhat surreptitiously to maintain their reasonable physical and psychiatric health so they could comprehend the crimes they had committed. There was one prisoner I counseled for a few weeks, discussing the details of his theft and the reasons for the punishment. After his original resistance and self-starvation, he came around to accepting his punishment with honor and integrity.

The special dining room and quarters on a separate deck for the pilots kept them working closely together as they knew each other's habits and personalities extremely well. They were all good-looking, cocky, and fun loving, but had no window to look out over the ocean, except for the flight deck, which was dangerous. The only place with an ocean view was the library, where I spent much of my off-duty time reading Japanese Renaissance literature.

Chapter Twenty-Eight

A Bad Business Deal

I was always reluctant to involve myself with Koreans in America, since they seemed to live in too isolated and cliquish a manner, too bound by their language and customs—but calls kept coming requesting my attendance at Korean community meetings, as I had become a somewhat high-profile figure in the community, having received some awards for various service, and professional accomplishments. I finally accepted a membership to their board of the Korean American Association of Seattle, but declined the nomination for the position of president due to concerns I had doubt about the purpose of the organization, which showed warning signs of corruption from the onset of my involvement with them. I also questioned their relationship to the Korean government when I noticed that the South Korean president came to meet with the board members in Seattle.

Around 1990 when the AT&T monopoly was broken, there was interest in forming a telephone company to deliver calls between the US and Korea. Ten luminaries with deeper pockets and creative entrepreneurial vision raised over a million dollars to establish a full-scale telephone exchange company similar to MCI. There were only two people capable of running the company: myself and a local Washington state representative. After many discussions, I agreed to help create the company, stopped taking new patients, and devoted the majority of my time to this project, and even hired an American telephone expert, promising him generous stock options for his help. He and I studied in the evenings, and after a month or two identified the proper switching equipment and went to Texas to buy it. We brought it back to Seattle and installed it in a high-rise next to the Westin hotel, where all the Seattle telephone lines converged. Soon there were thousands of subscribers to "TTI," Transpacific Telecom Incorporated.

I. DAVID HONG MD, US NAVY CAPTAIN, RETIRED

The problems began with the ever-increasing greed of the core participants. I was not paid a dollar, and my American expert was later denied his stock options through a vote of the board of directors. The Korean government agent on the board wanted complete control, something totally unexpected. The most culpable party was the state representative, Paul Shin, since he had more interest than all the rest. It just so happens that Kim's brother married Shin's sister. Shin seemed to have a secret agenda with the Korean government, which had worried me from the start. I resigned and went back to my medical practice since I was not paid nor given the promised stock options. I also quit attending board meetings, but saw in the correspondences among them much distrust, dishonesty, and secret collusions to dominate the company at the expense of others. Finally, the company seemed to give in but would not accept Frontier Telephone Company's offer to buy them out, which I had recommended. In the end, everybody lost; and the company went bankrupt. I made a legal motion against the board of directors to recover my promised salary, which I finally won after much expense. They paid out of their pockets, and the matter was ended. The Korean American Association of greater Seattle also was subsequently dissolved into insignificance for the better.

Meanwhile Mother had moved to Pusan, having donated one million dollars to a Christian organization founded by several doctors and ministers to buy a four-story building overlooking Pusan Harbor. Because of her progressive Alzheimer's disease in the early 1990s, I made several trips there to assist in her medical treatment, including attempts to bring her to the US to get better medical attention. At the last minute, before boarding for America, Aida, her maid persuaded her to stay in Korea and abort her departure. Her dependents did not want to lose her and had a strange selfish grip on her. Later I heard from a representative of Yuhan Corporation that she had donated all her assets to various organizations. One of her nephews from Seoul, whom I had seen three times since 1956, sought her out in Pusan with an attorney and a medical doctor, and got her to sign over all of her assets to Yonsei University, where the nephew was employed. Shortly after that, he was announced as the department chair at the medical school there! She, the attorney, and the doctor were all hailed the next morning in the Seoul newspapers for their selfless sacrifice to Korean society. Years later, I met the doctor and the attorney who certified my mother's mental competence. While they agreed privately that she was mentally incompetent, they said, "it was good for society" and they were "honored to partake in the endowment."

Mother had rejected all of the Hong family, all of her four kids, since she blamed the failure of their marriage on my father, and thus saw herself as shamed in the eyes of society. She was a narcissist with inflated ideas of her own importance, and weakened by her need for admiration and public recognition and adoration—seemingly always at the overt expense of others nearby. At Mother's funeral, Julie, my youngest sister met Aida for the first time in fifty years who confessed to her then that Mother had offered her a large sum of money to take Julie, then two years old, to the countryside and raise her as her own child, but Aida had declined. Julie was certainly the Cordelia of the three daughters, though Misa was similarly mistreated.

CHAPTER TWENTY-NINE

Final Mission in Guatemala

In 1997 I volunteered for a jungle medical expedition with the Navy Seals deep in Guatemala, one hundred miles northeast of Guatemala City to help guerilla groups oppose the Communists, and to rally the locals to our cause and increase their morale. A month before my deployment, I applied for the required diplomatic passport and arrived at the Guatemala airport, met by embassy personnel with the other expedition members. We were ushered through the back door without going through customs and picked up by a partially armored vehicle with darkened windows. There was metal mesh in the glass to stop projectiles. I was a little afraid, but we met all our companions at the US embassy and went to our hotels. I stayed in the Westin with the instructions to meet the following morning at 6:00 a.m. for further instructions before departing for the mission. Among our soldiers, there was talk about the fragile situation in Guatemala, as there was a lot of pro-Communist activity against the Guatemalan government, which we were backing, similar to the Sandinistas in Nicaragua

The next morning, we boarded a caravan of SUVs, each large enough for four soldiers with baggage and proceeded north for six hours, finally arriving at the headquarters of the northern Guatemalan army base where we spent the night. We were given a special reception by the Guatemalan generals and some of us were invited to a crude but effective sauna made from scrap metal. They piped boiling water in from an outside heater to make a shower where we could relax with a beer. We slept well and prepared for the commencement of the mission the next day.

We then drove several hours further north into the mountains. This time the Navy Seals rode fully armed at the front vehicle ready to counterattack if necessary—a somewhat disconcerting sight. At the front of the caravan was a

Mercedes truck with twenty Guatemalan soldiers, also fully armed, followed by a supply truck. I was in the third car in the back seat. The Guatemalan soldiers guided us northward toward the Santa Rosa Mountain range. We drove higher into the mountains on some nasty roads, taking an extreme drop into the jungle abyss. One driving mistake and it would be impossible to retrieve a truck from the sharp incline below. At midday we passed, what we were told was an American missionary compound a block off of the road. An American priest who was sympathetic to the indigenous Communist natives was killed there by the Guatemalan government soldiers because he was hiding Communists and providing them with information and supplies. Finally, just before sunset, we arrived at a large school-like building. In the auditorium, we arranged our sleeping bags and cots. To take a shower the next morning, we had to walk a block to a civilian running water system that had been arranged just for us. As we walked to the showers, the Guatemalan troops watched and protected us.

We brought a truckload of medical supplies with us, including antibiotics, injectable medication, veterinary medicines, portable surgical equipment, and even dental chairs. We soon found that most of the locals never had dental care in their lives. We moved to a new village every two days. Remote villagers would walk long distances from every direction to get treatment for their families and animals. Early one morning, we found a line of a few hundred people waiting to see us. The most common complaint was severe headaches from parasites contracted through bad drinking water. Their well was being contaminated, as they had no sewer system. We did not bring any chemicals to put into the well, which I thought we should have done. Even Clorox would have done the job. I saw so many patients in an endless stream all day long each day, including removing a neuroma from a woman's foot that had prevented her from wearing shoes. On the other side of the hill, veterinarians treated cows, working horses, and goats. The dental line was also long, as most of the people had infected teeth that needed to be pulled. Some were totally toothless by the time they left the clinic. I was proud again to be an American and believed then as I do now that the only way to gain the sympathy of people is by providing real help with their most pressing problems, just as we were doing. This builds trust and creates true diplomacy, the only way to cultivate political allies. A much better way to create allies is to show humanitarian goodwill before troubles and dispossessed people have reason to become our adversaries. I remember what the Americans had done for the people in Korea; and it certainly converted me and my family to befriend America, as opposed to the Chinese; though I'll never forget that Chinese soldier at the Han River Bridge who selflessly gave my father and me his day's rations when we were so hungry.

Meanwhile I received word that arrangements had been made for two physicians who missed the plane to arrive by helicopter 150 miles from Belize to the northeast. I learned then that we had a significant presence, called Southern Command throughout the Americas all the way down to Tierra del Fuego. We gathered for a rendezvous with two late arrivals at the top of the hill. Looking down from the hill, all you could see was jungle canopy like a green eternity to the horizon. I remembered the trip with Sharon years ago through the remote jungle roads in this area—something that might be impossible to do safely now. In a short time, we heard a plane approaching with increasing noise. The helicopter landed on the mountain and dropped off two additional physicians to join our crew. This was the same place that high command had designated as the landing point should we be overwhelmed by enemy forces and need to evacuate. It reassured me to know that such a plan existed.

In the evenings, we were often invited to village events and celebrations and socialized with the people we were aiding while learning their customs. I even bought souvenirs—some fine Guatemalan weavings and bead art. My Spanish lessons also came in handy here as I was able to exchange some thoughts and give some simple gifts to a few of the people.

Every evening at 9:00, a young captain put up an antenna and communicated with his command in Belize, discussing the day's activities and receiving new orders. After about ten days, we returned in the same formation through the same road out of the jungle, still wary of possible attacks.

Chapter Thirty

Reflections of an "Elder"

As I venture through my late sixties now, retired and taking time to travel and experience the world with Kim, I continue to incur challenges, the most recently of infirmity, the onset of a not-so-rare autoimmune disease where now allergic to his own cells. As my journey continues, even with these limitations and aches and pains of the body, I have noticed that the spirit *does not* age; it feels just the same as it did when I was a child. The sound of rushing water in the creek in my backyard is just as enchanting as it was when I was a boy fishing on the Han River, or the first time I fly-fished high in the Sierras. I still feel liberated by the sound of violins in a symphony or an exquisite aria, still feel touched by the chorus of birds in the Washington summer mornings, and often have to remind myself that I am almost an old man. I simply do not feel that way most of the time, though not long ago a doctor told me I could expire at any time. The heart of a child still beats within me, and I take it with me everywhere I go.

I cannot help but often think about the welfare of children in our country who are struggling under oppressive circumstances, much neglect, and risk that accompanied my formative years in foster homes. Ultimately, it was the care and kindness of the multiple staff members with whom one could relate in an orphanage that gave me opportunities to blossom from ashes a new life.

Children become orphaned and displaced for a variety of reasons. In my case, I believe it was my destiny that I am part of all whom I have met from the past while the guardian angels always seemed to hover from THE ABOVE.

Typically, when you mention orphanages to Americans, they think of destitution and conjure squalid images of filth and poverty—or other Charles Dickens-like cliché's. The truth is that we need orphanages more now, not

I. DAVID HONG MD, US NAVY CAPTAIN, RETIRED

foster care homes which is very confining to growth as was in my case of living with a couple like the Gilmores, who would have certainly interfered with my development and prevented me from attaining my dreams. Instead, with the good fortune of in an orphanage, the guides like the Silverthornes, Mr. Howe, and others gave me multiple surrogates and opportunities to encounter, develop, find my distinct identity, and do something very special with my life ...

I am a true fruits of the Great American experiment and that the only limitations that ultimately existed were those I set for myself.

As a psychiatrist and a lifelong student of human behavior, and in witnessing the turns of my own life, I have concluded that most all loss of direction and inner turmoil stems from an individual's reaction to their perceived inadequacies, be they real or imagined.

At the end, it is in struggling one finds meaning and sees himself for the first time.

It has been an exhilarating journey indeed into my golden years, less my AB42 peptide of 644 presses further.

1946 : Me and my sisters in motherless years with two Aunts.

1955 : The Scarecrow Hut by the countryside,
before departing to Pusan Harbor

後世稍誰大丈夫、失信不立他鄉逸
男兒二十未平國、
頭蒲江水飲馬無高眼手穿花崗聞花港
白頭山石磨刀盡饑不擇食故國思
日暮途遠重青更來

至情所發 勞人心動. 管鮑之交 晴平不再來
修身齊家治國平天下 過則勿憚改 過猶不及
己所不欲 勿施於人 士為知己者死 巧言分色
改乎寒端 斯害也已 獅子身中之虫 不恥不問
朋友有信 思相疑 不覺淚下 上濁下不淨
長幼有序 同伴絕 解散絕
夫婦有別 三八絕
父子有親 民主絕
君臣有義 曉夢甚煩 修人事待天命
五倫: 心懷極惡 成大功者不小苟

男兒之句出鄉關
學若不成死不還

1955: Ninth Grade, my calligraphy on Confucius Teachings.

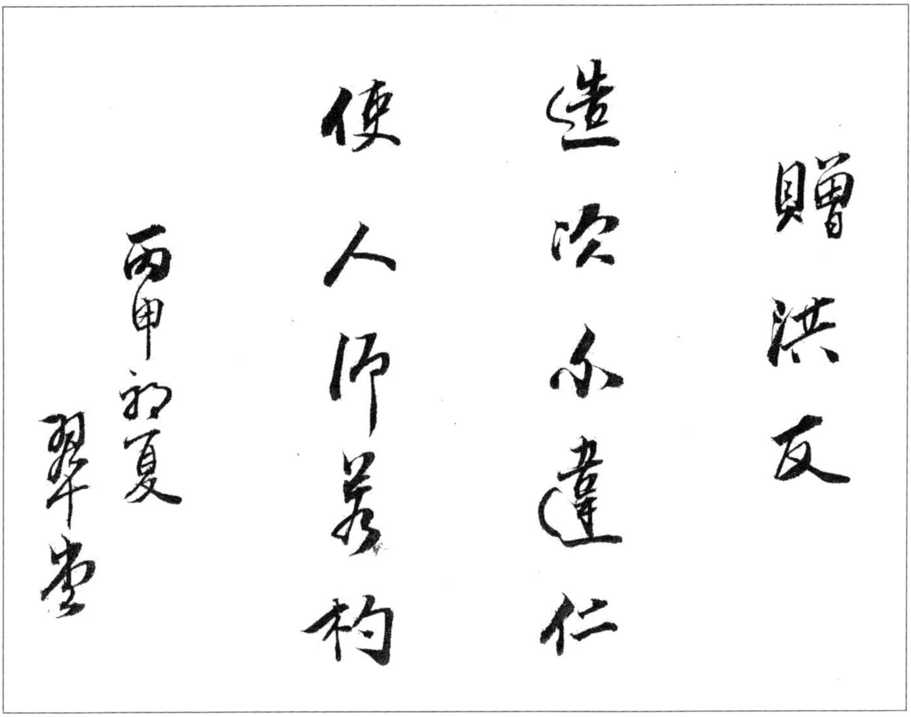

贈洪友

造次必違仁
使人所芳杓

丙申初夏
翠堂

1956 : My teacher's departing message to me.

1956: Departing to America

1956: On the way to San Francisco.

1957-1960: Spanish American Institute Orphanage

September 15, 1957. ~ September 22, 1957 "The first day in S.A.I"

It was an evening when we left home. But I still didn't know where I was going. But I have a will and I will follow in God. I extended. Kindly after long curiosity I arrived Spanish American Institute. I was glad. Now I am free. Now I am able to find real America behind hard-hearted. Now I stay in here. But I was remembering what my father said, "Mr. Koreans can be concerned to you," and "Put my hand on with to promise not to do certain thing such as not to go out. First impression on S.A.I was rather good even though I was disappointed when I saw a dirty room. Roommate. We decorated by ourselves all the things — our room. Showed me all my accommodation. Looks were made four our storage. In cafeteria I ate plenty, as much as I want. I got up at 5:30 and work until 9:00. and go to bed about after eleven o'clock. But I don't feel tired. I feel strong. I worked in the office on the other day and Mrs. Silverton gave me some clothes as well as David, one of my friend. All of them were awfully nice to me. As I came out to study. I study as much as I want, perhaps six or six hours a day. I am doing fine even in poor apparatus. Teacher are always nice to me. I took Physics, U.S. History, English, gym, chemistry, and U.S. Gov't. School was brand new with all new accommodation. House mother, Miss Pope-me lended me a loud (electric) for my studying. There is a television in living room, however, I seldom watch television. I spend more time in reading and studying. I am glad that I came out but still I won't be able to see my sister, neither others whom I want see. But I know they are all well as I spoke to them. They were awfully nice and give me most economic help. I thanked them in my letter. I had my letters from Korea. But I just can't help their gratitude. And their loving heart toward me. They are going to send me some money too. I can work coordinator to find a job, but I can't leave foster mother I want. Why I don't know. Today I was the receptionist in our office offered on Sunday. And I prayed before lunch in our dining room for our dinner. Boys recommended me as a rather mature. But I don't feel that I am old enough or able to manage quite well. But it is my understanding that I want and try my best as I can if I want. Today my (2) forester parents came in here and visited me. I was glad but not embarrassed. They tried to me nice to me. And I am tried too. But her way of talking was still and never be all right. By this time about 12 o'clock I finished all my work and ready to work in my favorite school.

September 1957: First series of diaries on the arrival at the orphanage.

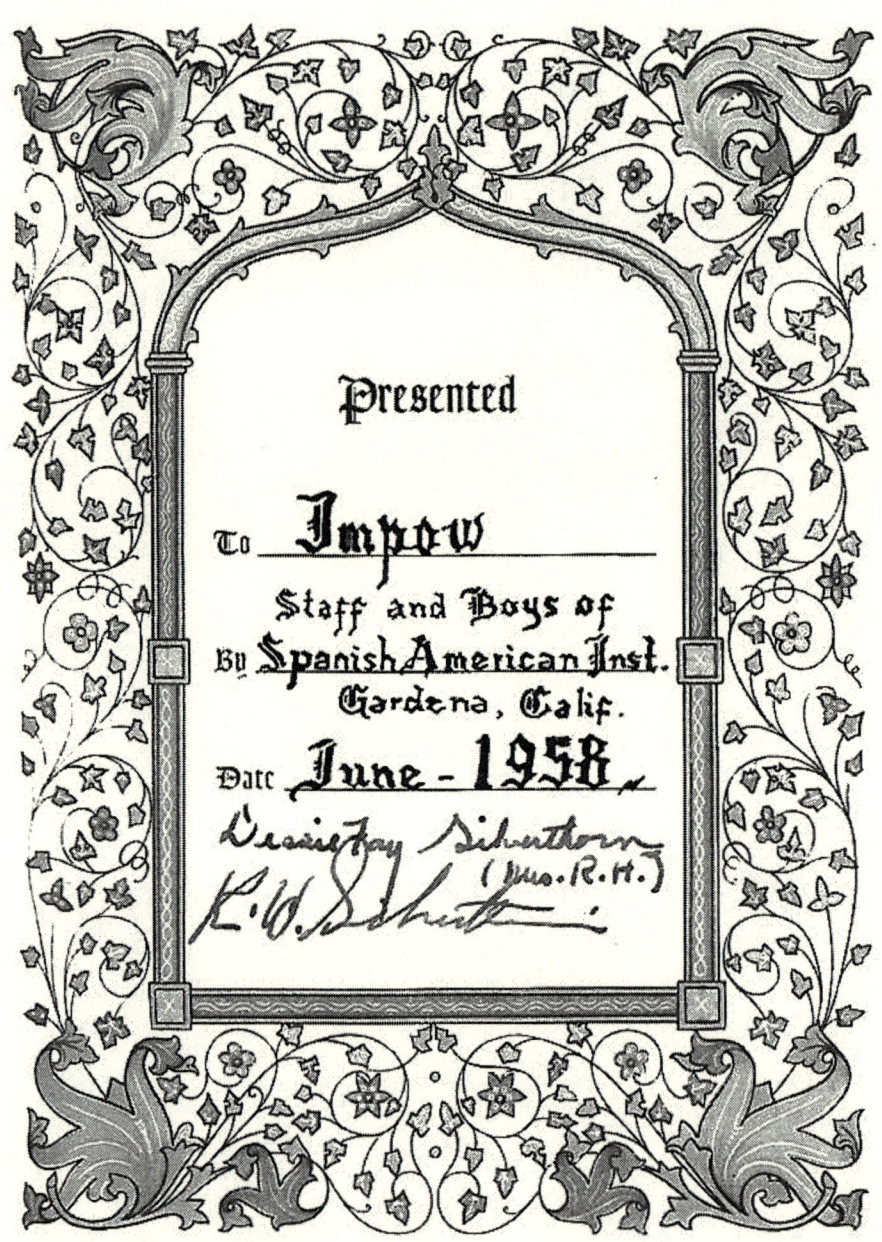

1958: The bible presented to me by the Director of the orphanage on my baptism at the chapel.

Certificate of Baptism

THIS IS TO CERTIFY —
that in the Name of the Father and of the Son and of the Holy Spirit

Inpow Gilmore

was baptized on the _23_ day of _March_, 19_58_.

NAME OF CHURCH HERE
"_Chapel of Friendship_"   R. H. SILVERTHORN, Minister

1958: The Orphanage Director, Dr. Silverthorn and me

1959: SAI Orphanage Christmas Service, me as a wiseman

1959: Me in California Migrant Ministry

California Migrant Ministry

I. ntroduction.
 A. Appreciation of speech.
 B. My topic announcement
 C. Education of foreign student
 d. Minority of Americans (purpose — in form)
II. Situation of Migrants. (in America, emphasis)
 A. Who are they
 B. Origin.
 C. Composition.
 d. Occupation.
 e. Social standing
III. Standard of living
 A. House facility. & sanitation — Tooth paste, soap.
 B. Children.
 C. Movement — 6 time in a year
 e. Clothes, food,
IV. Need of these people. Education — white 18 years
 A. Need of education.
Last 1. illiteracy, Truman.
   2. Buying a pump for flat tire
   3. Reason:
    Too many children.
    Too many movement
 → B. Recognition.
 C. Security
 D. Understanding & love, Burbank

1959: The outline for the 11 A.M. Sunday church
services speech on Migrant Ministry

Alpha Gamma Sigma

This is to certify that

INPOW HONG

has been elected to permanent membership in the California Junior College Honor Scholarship Society and is entitled to all the rights and privileges pertaining thereto

Tau — CHAPTER
June 17, 1960 — DATE
Compton College — COLLEGE
Esther Conrad — ADVISER
President

UNIVERSITY OF SOUTHERN CALIFORNIA
LOS ANGELES 7

Office of the Dean of Students   Award No. 1280

Mr. Inpow Hong
P.O.Box 272
Gardena, California

June 8, 1960

Notice of Award of Scholarship

Dear Mr. Hong:

In recognition of your high academic achievement and outstanding school citizenship, the University of Southern California is pleased to award you a scholarship for **full tuition for the year 1960-61, for not less than fourteen nor more than eighteen units per semester.**
The Committee on Student Aid has recommended you for this award. It is effective beginning **September 1960** and is renewable up to a maximum of eight undergraduate semesters. The continuation of your scholarship depends upon the excellence of the record you make in the University.

Awards apply to the day division (University Park) and do not cover more than one course per semester in classes taken at University College or Civic Center.

Because of the unusual demand for scholarships, you are requested to reply to this letter not later than **June 27, 1960** indicating whether or not you accept this award. If we do not hear from you by that time, we will assume that you are unable to accept and will reassign this scholarship. If you accept, please preserve this letter for presentation at the time of your registration.

Should you receive a California State Scholarship or any other scholarship grant in addition to this award, the University of Southern California will adjust its award to reflect the improvement of your financial status.

With the hope that you will accept this scholarship and join us at SC, I am

Sincerely yours,

ROBERT J. DOWNEY
Dean of Students

Type of scholarship granted........**Pond**..*

*Service scholarships entail a definite number of hours in service to the University. If your award is of service type, please report after you have registered to the Scholarship Office, Student Union 328, for assignment.

The University of
Southern California
March 23, 1962

Mr. Indow Hong
7011 Vine Vale
Bell, California

Dear Mr. Hong:

We are very pleased to notify you that you have been elected to membership in Alpha Epsilon Delta, National Premedical Honor Society, and we hope that you will accept.

Since the time before the initiation banquet is short, please reply as quickly as possible to:
    Prof. Walter E. Martin
    Department of Biology
    University of Southern California

                Sincerely yours,

                Walter E. Martin

                For Alpha Epsilon Delta

Accepted

1960: The Compton College Transcript.

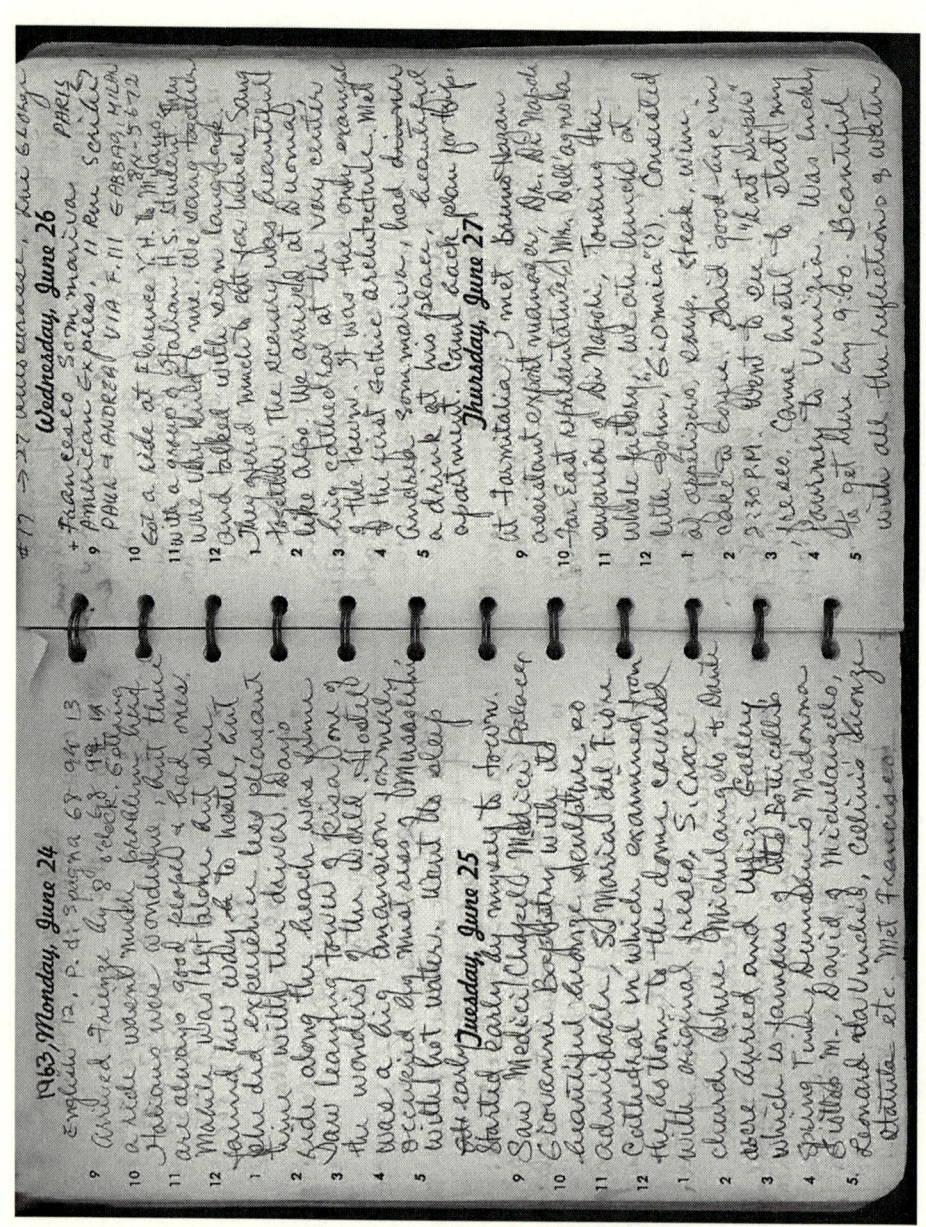

1963: Notes for the Around The World Tour.

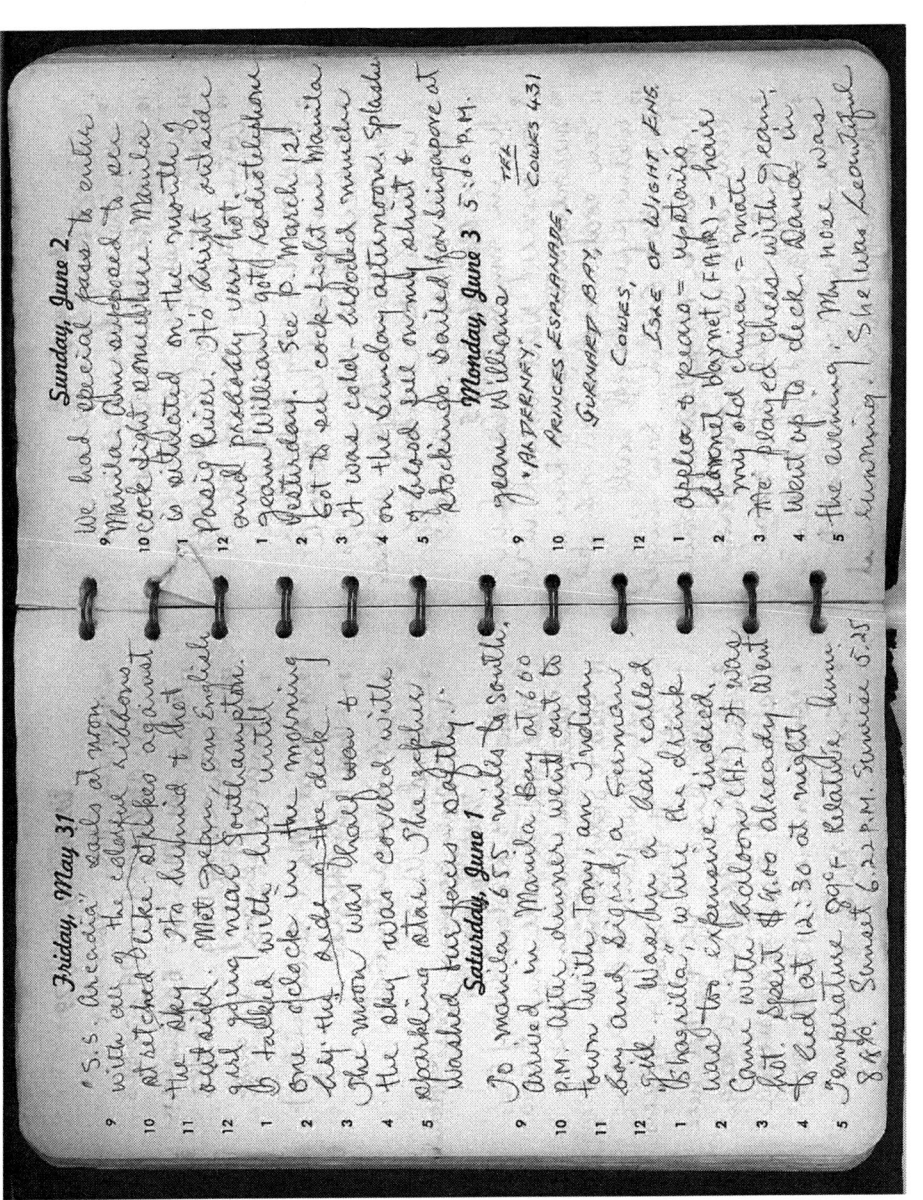

1963: Notes for the Around The World Tour.

1963: Me on Camel ride to the Pyramid of Giza

PASSENGER CARRYING PROHIBITED

A violation of this limitation may result in the REVOCATION FOR ONE YEAR of this certificate or any pilot certificate subsequently issued.

UNITED STATES OF AMERICA – FEDERAL AVIATION AGENCY

STUDENT PILOT CERTIFICATE

This Certifies That: (Full name and address) INPOW HONG 836 BATTLEFIELD DRIVE NASHVILLE TENNESSEE 37204

CERTIFICATE NO. S- 5569

DATE OF BIRTH	HEIGHT	WEIGHT	HAIR	EYES	SEX	NATIONALITY
10-30-40	68 IN.	150	BLACK	BROWN	M	USA

is properly qualified to exercise the privileges of a Student Pilot.

This certificate is temporary for a period of 90 days; if no notice to the contrary is received within such period, it will remain in effect until the expiration date shown below, unless otherwise ordered by the Federal Aviation Agency.

LIMITATIONS

Passenger Carrying Prohibited.

GLIDER

ISSUANCE DATE 4-27-67

EXPIRATION DATE 4-30-69

By Direction of the Administrator

SIGNATURE OF EXAMINER OR INSPECTOR GARLAND W. PACK

EXAM. DESIG. NO. OR INSPECTOR'S REG. NO. 080/5PEG

DATE EXAMINER'S DESIG. EXPIRES: 8-31-67

SIGNATURE OF STUDENT PILOT

FEDERAL AVIATION AGENCY UNITED STATES OF AMERICA

FORM FAA-340 (5-58)

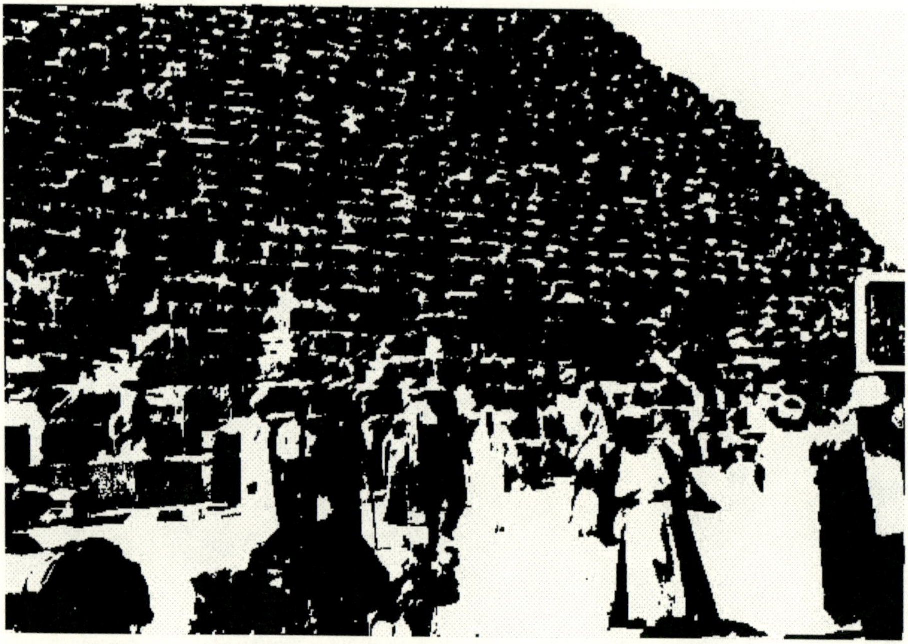

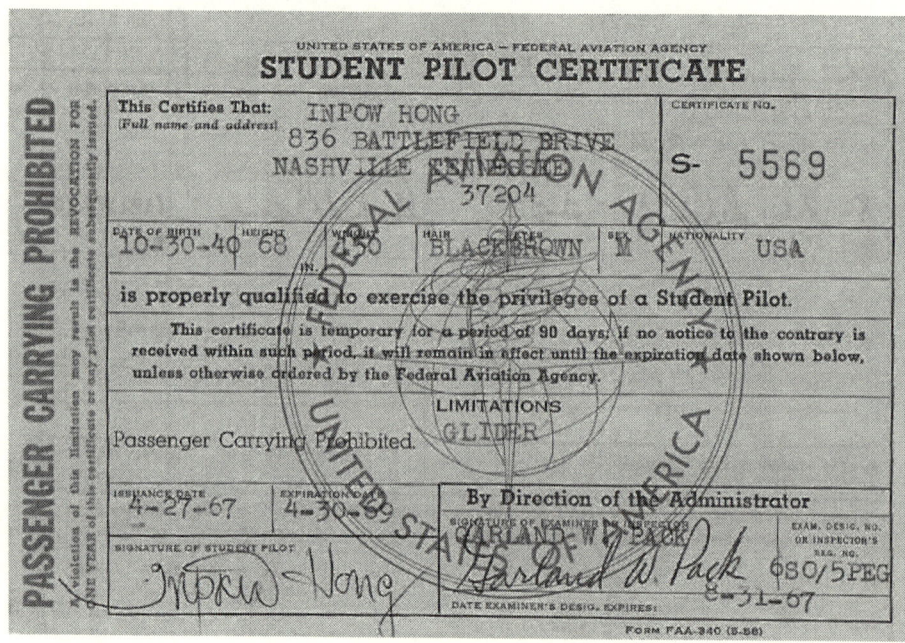

24 March '67
Seoul

J. Hong
836 Battlefield Dr
Nashville, Tenn.   (Copy to Yong Gak)

仁約아 지금 쯤 너에게 着地 쯤이면 韓國에서 색시는
마음대로 골라잡을판이고 아버지생각에는 좋은 家門에서 높은 敎養
을 받은 特히 머리좋은 (뿌레반이 사-B 한) 색시를 며누리로 맞아들여서
한국적 가정을 이룩해 아버지의 맏아들로 태여나

1 祖上 (조상)도 성실이 받들고
3 아버지의 死後라도 (죽은뒤에라도) 새엄마를잘 奉養 (봉양) 하며
   비록 배 다른 동생이라도 아버지에게는 너나똑같은 아들이니 불상한 어린동생
   준호를잘 養育해서 장차 榮華롭게 성가 (成家) 싶여주도록 바라는
   마음 目眦에도 (잠시반시라는듯) 잊혀못할만큼 간절하였으며
   또 아버지가 맏이면큰아들인 너를 안믿고 누구에게 희망걸겠느냐
   그런 돈찬이 되고 네 편지로는 Darlene 과 결혼이틀림없으니 아버지
   내 큰 심이 노이지 안는다 며누리를 맞는다는 기쁜 반면 우리집안 꼴이 엉박이되겠
   도대체가 묘地께 집을 너에게 相續 (상속) 이란 根本的으로
   말도 안 되는것이나 아버지생각은 너석均를 중심으로한 韓國고유
   의 가족제도를 꿈꾸엇기때문인데 지금와서는 外國시민권을
   가진 사람에게는 상속도되지 안고 아버지기대 에는 너무 달나젔음으
   1963 한국와서 아버지와 약속하였든 집의 상속문제는 완전히취소
   (Cancelle) 하니 너도 그리 알어라
   지금 상태 아버지도 살지는 못할것같다
                              너무 피곤해서 이만 쓴다
   (아버지는 네가 집에대하야
   말이 있을때 내주라고 우편으로
   부쳐 반고 작은 아버지에게
   맡겨 두엇다 Y.S.H)   Y.S. Hong

1967: My Father's last letter to me

1973: Hunting on my 130-acre Farm, Columbia Tennessee

By the Honorable
JOHN S. WILDER
Speaker of the Senate and Lieutenant Governor

Greetings: Be it hereby known that

___DR. INPOW HONG___

in recognition of outstanding service to the state, and extraordinary interest in Governmental processes has been appointed

An Honorary Member
of the Lieutenant Governor's Staff

and is hereby entitled to all of the honors and privileges of the office, and to the display of this certificate

Given under my hand, this

___12___ *day of* ___MARCH, 1974___

JOHN S. WILDER
SPEAKER OF THE SENATE
AND
LIEUTENANT GOVERNOR

1974

1999-2000: Homecoming after hunting excursion

2000: Me in Medical Expedition into Guatemalan jungle, Santa Rosa area, with the Navy Seals

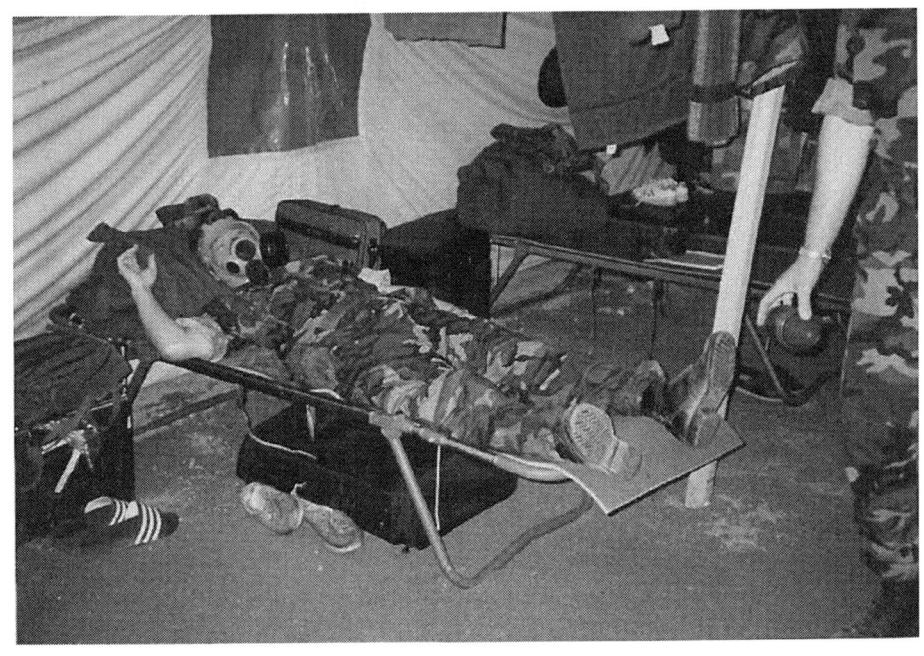

2000: Sleeping in tent with gas mask during Guatemalan Expedition.

AMERICAN BOARD OF
PSYCHIATRY & NEUROLOGY

I. David Hong, M. D.
CABRINI TOWERS, SUITE 707
901 BOREN AVE.
SEATTLE, WA 98104

TEL. (206) 587-5747

CURRICULUM VITAE
MAY 1999, Retired 2001

1. Name: Hong, Inpow David

2. Residence: 2535 Medina Circle
Medina, WA. 98039   Tel: (425) 454-8550
                     Fax: (425) 455-3633
                     E-Mail: idhong@earthlink.net
From 1980 - Present

3. Office: Cabrini Medical Tower   Tel: (206) 587-5747
           901 Boren Avenue, Suite 707 Fax: (206) 682-5267
           Seattle, WA. 98104   Pager: (206) 570-5705
                                      E-Mail: idhong@earthlink.net
From 1980 - present Retired 2001

4. Birthplace & Date: Born in Seoul, Korea on Oct. 30, 1940; Immigrated to U.S. 1956

5. Citizenship: U.S.A. ; Social Security No: available on request

6. Marital Status: Wife: Kim Hong ; Children: Alexander, Lisa and Robert

7. Education: Gardena High School, Gardena, CA. 1958
              University of Southern California, B.S. Cum Laude, 1962
              Vanderbilt Medical School, M.D., Nashville, TN, 1967
   Internship: USPHS Hospital, Rotating, Boston, Mass., 1967-68
   Residency: USPHS, NIMN, Intramural Training, Washington D.C., 1969-71
               Vanderbilt Hospital, Nashville, Tenn., 1971-72

8. Professional   Administrative Physician, PHS, NIMH, Clinical Research Center
   Experience: Fort Worth, Texas, 1968-69
                  Director, Drug & Alcohol Rehabilitation Center,
                     Central State Hospital, Nashville, Tenn. 1972-73
                  Private Practice in Adult Psychiatry, 1973-78
                     634 Medical Arts Bldg., Nashville, Tenn. 37212
                  Chief, Alcohol Treatment Facility, 1978-80
                     121st Evacuation Hospital (Seoul, Korea)
                     APO, San Francisco, CA. 96301
                  Private Practice in Adult Psychiatry at same address above
                     1980 - Present, 2001

9. Diplomat in American Board of Psychiatry & Neurology, 1978, #17446

10. Professional Interest: Acute Adult Psychiatry, Psychosis and Bipolar Disorders

11. Professional Honors: Clinical Associate Professor in Psychiatry,
                         University of Washington, 1980-84

	Chairman, Department of Psychiatry, Cabrini Hospital Seattle, WA. 1989-91
	Chairman, Washington State Korean Medical Dental Association 1989-91
12. Other Honors:	Vice-Chairman, Seattle-Washington Korean Association
	Board of Trustees, American-Korea Friendship Society, John Spellman, President
	Founder and President, TTI Telecommunications, Seattle, WA
	U.S. Navy, Officer Promotion Selection Committee
13. Service:	USPHS 1967-1971
	U.S. Army 1978-1980
	Captain, U.S. Naval Reserves 1990- Retired 2002 with
14. Hobbies:	Golfing - Member, Overlake Country Club, Skiing, Glider Pilot, International Traveling
15. Prof. Memberships:	Washington State Psychiatric Association
	American Psychiatric Association
	38th Parallel Medical Association
	North Pacific Society of Neurology and Psychiatry
	King County Medical Society
16. Medical Licenses:	State of Tenn.1970, State of WA.1978, State of CA.1971
17. Staff Privileges:	Providence Medical Center, Seattle, WA., 1980-Present
18. References:	

Glenn T. Strand, M.D. 901 Boren Ave., Suite, 707, Seattle, WA. 98104, Tel. 682-4406
  Clinical Assoc. Professor, University of Washington, Psychiatry Department
  Ex-President, N.W. Pacific Neurology & Psychiatry Society
  Ex-President, Seattle Chapter, American Psychiatric Association
Robert Orenstein, M.D. 901 Boren Ave., Suite 1333, Seattle, WA. 98104, Tel. 623-7444
  Clinic Associate Professor, University of Washington.
Robert Olsen, M.D. 1101 Madison #1216, Seattle, WA. 98104, Tel. 622-5455
  Ex-Chairman, Providence Hosp, Psych. Dpt., Clinic Assoc. Professor, Univ. of WA.
Philip Lindsay, M.D. 1101 Madison, Seattle, WA. 98104, Tel. 622-5454
Steve Shimizu, C.P.A., 1601 116th Ave. NE #111, Bellevue,WA. 98004
Steve Funk, Attorney, 10900 NE 8th Street, Suite 850, Bellevue, WA. 98004 Tel 425-455-5100

DR. & MRS. I. DAVID/KIM HONG
TEL 4254548550/FX 455-3633
E - IDHONG@EARTHLINK.NET
2535 MEDINA CIR
MEDINA, WA 98039-1503

2002: Gliding in Whistler, Canada

2003: My wife and me cruising around the South America, Pentagonia, Strait of Magellan

2004: Ephesus, Turkey, Temple of Artemus

2005: New Year celebration with my wife Kim, Lisa and Robert

2006: Home of 28 years in summer and winter